Launchpad

Text copyright © Neil Pugmire and Mark Rodel 2004
Illustrations copyright © Baz Rowell 2004
Musical arrangements copyright © Kevin Golledge 2004
The authors assert the moral right
to be identified as the authors of this work

Published by
The Bible Reading Fellowship
First Floor, Elsfield Hall
15–17 Elsfield Way, Oxford OX2 8FG

ISBN 1 84101 326 9
First published 2004
10 9 8 7 6 5 4 3 2 1 0
All rights reserved

Acknowledgments
Unless otherwise stated, scripture quotations are taken from the Contemporary English Version of the Bible published by HarperCollins Publishers, copyright © 1991, 1992, 1995 American Bible Society.

Scripture quotations taken from the Good News Bible published by The Bible Societies/HarperCollins Publishers Ltd, UK © American Bible Society 1966, 1971, 1976, 1992, are used with permission.

Performance and copyright
The right to perform *Launchpad* drama material is included in the purchase price, so long as the performance is in an amateur context, for instance in church services, schools or holiday club venues. Where any charge is made to audiences, written permission must be obtained from the authors, who can be contacted through the publishers. A fee or royalties may be payable for the right to perform the script in that context.

A catalogue record for this book is available from the British Library

Printed and bound in Malta

Launchpad

Seventeen child-centred service outlines
for all-age worship

Neil Pugmire and Mark Rodel

ACKNOWLEDGMENTS

Thanks to all those who've contributed to the development of the material in this book. Special thanks to past members of the 'Powerhouse' team at Tangier Road Baptist Church, Portsmouth—Sue Smith, Kevin and Ruth Leech, Alwyn Huteson, Martyn Philbrick and Karen Cray, Gill Cray, and Giles and Jane Tewkesbury. Members of the *Launchpad* team at St Jude's, Southsea—Paul Nelson, Chris and Abbie Richardson, Eirené Rouse, Jane Fardon, Andrea Murray and Sarah Williams—also played a crucial part in shaping this material. The congregations and clergy at both churches, especially Richard Hardy and John Byrne, gave decisive support and encouragement. Many children have also influenced us with their enthusiasm to join in music, drama and activities.

Thanks also to Richard Landall for allowing us to borrow the name of the Sunday morning children's groups at St Clare's, Park Barn, for this material.

Thanks also to our wives—Ann Pugmire, Barbara Rodel and Joy Golledge. Their ideas, inspiration, patience and encouragement have been crucial.

This book is dedicated to Elliott and Toby Rodel, Hannah and Lauren Golledge, and all the other children and young people it has been our joy to work with. Our prayer is that they may all encounter Christ through the dedication of those who seek to launch them into the Christian faith.

Contents

Foreword

In *Launchpad*, Neil Pugmire and Mark Rodel have produced a valuable tool for the 21st-century church. If you want to reach and teach children, reading this book and getting a *Launchpad* team together would be time well spent.

These materials have been used to good effect with children over a number of years. A *Launchpad* team doesn't have to be expert to start, and has a lot of fun working together.

Church leaders with other responsibilities can be encouraged to trust a mixed-age team to run with the *Launchpad* materials. They are well thought-out and have become an important means of effective ministry to children in our city church.

Canon John Byrne
Vicar, St Jude's Church, Southsea

The Launchpad concept

Many churches have tried the concept of 'all-age worship' in family services, and discovered that it is difficult to make sure they appeal to every generation. Most attempts end up with some elements designed for children and some for adults, rather than having all parts appealing simultaneously to everyone. Sometimes a 'family service' ends up being little more than normal Sunday morning worship with a few token children's songs. Children can still feel mostly uninvolved, while adults can find the switch from traditional liturgy to simple action songs unnerving.

Launchpad is aimed directly at five- to eleven-year-olds. The idea is to 'launch' children into the Christian faith by presenting the gospel in a clear, exciting and non-patronizing way. Adults who attend are clear that this is the aim, and children know that this is a service for them, not an awkward halfway house.

Focusing unashamedly on children, thinking creatively about the way ideas are presented and keeping the message simple often helps to communicate profound truths to the rest of the congregation as well. People discover new things about God that they may not have learnt in a more traditional service structure.

Here are some of the features of this approach.

A SENSE OF IDENTITY

In our brand-conscious era, it's helpful to have a strong identity. It's something different from 'normal church' that children can latch on to and tell their friends about. They can even advertise it at school by wearing T-shirts and badges.

The *Launchpad* logo (shown in black and white on page 9, or available to download in colour from www.launchpad-services.com) can be used extensively on banners, promotional material, T-shirts and badges. There is also a *Launchpad* theme song that can be sung at the beginning of each service, and the OHP acetates or PowerPoint slides can include the *Launchpad* logo.

You could give your services a different name but do something similar, with a logo of your own.

CONTINUITY

The *Launchpad* branding gives some continuity, but it can be reinforced by having a dedicated team leading each service, including a group of musicians.

It's also important to pursue themes through a series, rather than each being a stand-alone piece of worship. This means that teaching points can be reinforced from month to month. The services in this book are divided into thematic series of either three or five services. Each has various activities, characters or presentations in common that children will begin to recognize.

TEAM LEADERSHIP

The whole burden of leading *Launchpad* should not fall on one person. A group of people, perhaps half a dozen, should form a *Launchpad* team. Others can be brought in to help lead particular services, but a core group should be responsible for planning and leading. Ideally, these shouldn't be people who already lead Sunday School groups, as family services may be the only time such leaders get to worship with the rest of the congregation.

The guiding principle is that no one person should have a monopoly on leading worship, even if ordained ministers or trained children's workers have greater expertise. If we model such collaborative ministry to children, we may foster a sense of co-operation and empowerment among a new generation of church leaders.

In practical terms also, team leadership makes sense. In a team consisting mostly of volunteers, some may not be available for every service. And, because there is no one 'sermon' slot in *Launchpad*, different team members can present different segments without feeling daunted by preparing a whole 20-minute children's talk.

A STRONG VISUAL STYLE

We live in a visual age, yet often at church, speakers ask us to concentrate on sermon after sermon without giving any visual clues about their theme. No wonder we get bored! In *Launchpad*, little of the communication should be purely verbal. Each point should be illustrated by a visual aid, piece of drama, picture or activity. Even abstract spiritual points can be made with the help of illustrations, analogies or role-play.

There is no sermon in *Launchpad*. Teaching happens throughout the service in a variety of ways—taking part in an activity, singing a song, watching a presentation or answering questions. Service leaders are encouraged to draw out those teaching points from the various activities.

Multi-media presentation can also help to get the message across. This can include the use of OHP, sound effects, taped music and video. Many people will be familiar with the concept of song words or liturgical responses being projected on to screens using OHP. A data projector (usually connected to a laptop computer) simply takes this principle one step further: PowerPoint slides can be changed more smoothly and pictures can easily be incorporated in to the presentation. You can connect a video recorder to show video clips. Of course, much of the material in this book can also be used without such a projector.

CHILDREN SITTING AT THE FRONT

Children may already be familiar with the idea of sitting at the front of church with their friends, where they can see what is happening more easily. In a service that is devoted to them, such positioning is vital. It emphasizes the point that the service is for them, and it means that service leaders can interact with them and draw individuals out to take part in activities. It may be helpful to lay out carpet or cushions at the front to make the area more welcoming.

THE IMPORTANCE OF STORIES AND DRAMA

One of the best ways of communicating biblical truths is to dramatize them. This can mean performing a version of an actual Bible story, but it could also involve dramatizing real-life situations in which a principle can be applied. You don't need fantastic actors in your congregations. You can tell a story with congregational participation, use puppets, use narrators plus mime, or dress children up in costumes to re-enact a story. This book contains all those methods, as well as the obvious one in which team members take on characters and learn lines.

Drama can provide another way of ensuring continuity. Children will be keen to know what happens next to their favourite characters.

INVOLVING CHILDREN AND TEENAGERS

One of the best ways of exciting children and teenagers about a church service is to make sure they are involved—beyond being members of the congregation. This is especially helpful for those who are aged eleven and over, as the content of a *Launchpad* service is aimed at five- to eleven-year-olds.

Among the ways of involving them are:

- Asking a group of children, or a young family, to welcome people to the *Launchpad* service. They can wear *Launchpad* T-shirts and give out books and *Launchpad* badges.
- Asking a group of children (perhaps a particular children's Sunday group), or a family, to lead intercessory prayer. Ideally, the prayers should be written by the children or family beforehand.
- Asking one or more children to read Bible passages.
- Asking a children's Sunday group to prepare something before the service that is shared within *Launchpad* and contributes to its theme (perhaps a piece of artwork or a special reading).
- Playing instruments in the worship band.
- Involving teenagers in the drama pieces outlined in this book.

A RELEVANT APPLICATION OF THE BIBLE MESSAGE

Whatever the theme of the service, it's important that it leads to some kind of application for children at home or school. If, for instance, the message is that Christians should be 'lights of the world', the analogy should be explained in terms of what that means in the playground, or classroom, or when playing with friends. Ideally, the application should be something that families can talk about at home later.

SERVICES NO LONGER THAN 45 MINUTES

If you aim to finish your service within 45 minutes, then you at least stand a chance of making sure it lasts no longer than an hour! It's hard to get children under the age of 11 to concentrate for much longer than that, even if your service is full of exciting activities and fun action songs.

In this book, more material is presented for each session than would fit into a 45-minute service. Do pick out the songs, activities, drama and talks that you feel most comfortable with, rather than trying to do everything listed.

UNTHREATENING EVANGELISM

If children enjoy services at your church, they (and their parents) will feel comfortable inviting friends and family. They may wear *Launchpad* badges and T-shirts, promoting the brand name. *Launchpad* can become a way of evangelizing that is not heavy-handed. Invitations can be given to children in Sunday school who don't normally come to church, to uniformed organizations or to local primary schools. You may discover that new families become absorbed into the life of the church in a very unthreatening way.

The material can also be used in a holiday club context, with each service outline forming the basis of the main presentation each day for a three- or five-day event. It could even be adapted for use in school assemblies by resourceful churches or schools groups.

Launchpad

Preparing for Launchpad

In this book, you will find seventeen draft orders of service, which include suggested songs, activities, drama and segments of teaching. Use them as they stand, or adapt the material for your own needs.

The abbreviations in the text refer to the following books. For full details, see the bibliography on page 158.

GNB: Good News Bible (version 2)
KS: Kidsource
KS2: Kidsource 2
SOF: Songs of Fellowship
SOF2: Songs of Fellowship 2

You may not be in a position to stage some of the more complicated drama, produce *Launchpad* T-shirts and badges, or even manage to find half a dozen people from your congregation with the necessary skills to lead such services. Feel free to extract the material that you think would enhance your own services without necessarily embracing the *Launchpad* brand and all that it entails.

However, if you are planning to go for a complete *Launchpad*-style service, there are things you may need to do in preparation.

DRAW TOGETHER A TEAM

Allocate responsibilities for leading different parts of the service, publicizing it, photocopying scripts, leading drama and so on. Hold the first meeting several months before your first *Launchpad*. Many of the elements may need to be discussed with your church leadership.

PRODUCE BRANDED ITEMS

If you plan to use *Launchpad* T-shirts and badges, and to give out leaflets showing the *Launchpad* logo, this will take time to prepare. You can download a *Launchpad* logo to use on such items from www.launchpad-services.com or photocopy it from page 9. You will need to make sure you have enough T-shirts of various sizes for all the people leading the services, playing in the

music group, welcoming people, and so on. If you have *Launchpad* leaflets or a banner professionally made, this will also take some time.

PLAN PUBLICITY

Publicizing the change to your family services is vital—not least for the regular congregation. You can use leaflets initially for those within church, perhaps whetting their appetites with extracts from *Launchpad* material beforehand. If the congregation are excited by

the concept, they are more likely to tell others about it. Investigate whether you can go into local primary schools and lead assemblies on a *Launchpad* theme, then give out invitations for children to take home. Write a press release for the local newspaper, and offer to pose for photographs in costume. Put up a *Launchpad* banner outside the church. You could time your first *Launchpad* to run immediately after a holiday club, and include an item by the holiday club children within the service.

Posters, invitations and sample press releases are all available for you to download from www.launchpad-services.com.

LEARN THE LAUNCHPAD SONG

The *Launchpad* theme song is on pages 118–119. The idea is that it is sung at each *Launchpad* service to ensure continuity and provide a sense of anticipation for the children. Lead into the song with a countdown from 10 to 1, followed by 'Blast Off', alongside graphics showing an astronaut preparing to launch a rocket. The artwork on page 10 could be photocopied and displayed on an overhead projector. Alternatively, a flash animation sequence can be downloaded from www.launchpad-services.com.

You can create actions to go with the song. For example, children can pretend to take off like an aeroplane during 'We're gonna take off, fly high in the sky…' and leap into the air at the end of the line, 'Hey! Hey! We're on the Launchpad!' The *Launchpad* team could lead the singing and actions, to give a feeling that something special is going to happen.

DECORATE THE BUILDING AND / OR REARRANGE THE SEATING

If your church looks uninviting for children, why not make it look special for *Launchpad*? Perhaps a *Launchpad* banner could be hung at the front. What about some balloons or streamers?

You may have to reorganize some seating to fit in carpets or cushions at the front of the church. Do you want to make further changes to the seating for this service? Perhaps you could put the chairs in a semi-circle, or even move to the church hall, where children can sit more comfortably on the floor.

GOD'S HEROES

This five-part series follows schoolboys Billy Beefcake and Bertie Brainbox as they travel back in time to meet some of God's heroes from the Old Testament. In an age when children are looking for heroes, this series picks out the strengths and weaknesses of real-life characters who chose to follow God.

In the final episode, Billy and Bertie cross into the New Testament, promise to follow Jesus and are baptized by John the Baptist. They are disappointed not to meet God's ultimate hero, Jesus—but they return to the present day, discover that everyone in the whole congregation is actually one of God's heroes… and that they too can be God's heroes because they follow Jesus.

The characters studied, relevant Bible passages and teaching points are:

1. Joshua, the brave spy (Numbers 13:25–33; Joshua 1:1–9): God is with us when we feel scared and will help us.

2. Samuel, the obedient boy (1 Samuel 3:1–18; James 1:22–25): Listen to God and obey his instructions.

3. Esther, the courageous queen (Esther 2:19—7:10; Luke 10:30–35): Be brave and do the right thing.

4. Jonah, the reluctant prophet (Jonah 3:1—4:11; Matthew 5:43–48): God loves badly behaved people too.

5. John the Baptist (Mark 1:1–8): Follow Jesus!

An important element of this series is the 'time machine' in which Billy and Bertie travel. Don't worry if your church's budget won't stretch to convincing scenery or Hollywood-style special effects. It's possible to convey the impression by throwing a black cloth over a pulpit and attaching brightly-coloured buttons and switches. Alternatively, use a couple of chairs, a table and some computer or electrical equipment. For special effects, you could use a smoke machine or visual effects on a data projector, but they are not essential.

Joshua, the brave spy

 Teaching point

God is with us when we feel scared and will help us.

 Bible passages

Numbers 13:25–33; Joshua 1:1–9.

 Key verse

Don't ever be afraid or discouraged! I am the Lord your God, and I will be there to help you wherever you go.

JOSHUA 1:9

 Visual aids

Words or phrases for the activity on page 15 written out on separate cards.

SERVICE FRAMEWORK

★★★★★★★★★★★★★★★★★★★★★★★★★★★★★★
★   ★
★   **Welcome the congregation.**   ★
★   ★
★★★★★★★★★★★★★★★★★★★★★★★★★★★★★★

Give an explanation of *Launchpad* concept (if this is your first *Launchpad*).

Song

Sing the *Launchpad* song. (The congregation may have to learn it first.)

Talk outline

 The Bible has all sorts of stories in it about people who were chosen by God to do brave or exciting things to help him. We're going to meet some of those people in the next few *Launchpad* services.

Drama

God's heroes 1: Joshua *(see pages 16–19 for script)*.

Talk outline

 Recap the story of the Israelites and God's promise to them of a new land. Were there really giants in Canaan? The spies were just frightened of people they didn't know. God had promised them this land, but they were still scared when they saw the size and strength of the people living there. They felt that they were too small and weak to win against those people. Sometimes we feel a bit like that. We think we are too small and weak to do what God wants us to do, and we don't always trust him.

Confession

Dear Lord, please forgive us for the times we haven't trusted you. Give us the strength to do what you want. Amen.

Song

Everybody has a wobble (KS: 46)

Talk outline

 The other spies thought they were like an insect that could be squashed by giants. What was that insect? God says to us, like he said to the Israelites, 'You're not a grasshopper—small and weak. You're more like a giant—special and precious to me. And I've got great plans, if you trust me.'

Song

You may think I'm so young (KS: 397)

Talk outline

 What happened to the Israelites? As God said, they wandered in the desert for 40 years. Gradually, all the grown-ups got old and died, and the children grew up to be adults. After Moses died, God chose a new leader. Let's hear what happened. Listen out for God's promises.

Reading

Read Joshua 1:1–9.

Activity

 Before the service, distribute words and phrases from these promises around the church:

'No one will be able to stand up against you, all the days of your life.'

'I will never leave you or forsake you.'

'I will never abandon you.'

'The Lord your God will be with you wherever you go.'

Then say, 'God made some wonderful promises to Joshua. Let's see if we can find them around the church and put them back together.'

Talk outline

 Imagine how Joshua felt. He had seen this country 40 years ago and believed that God would give it to them. But God still had to say to him, 'Be strong and courageous.' Although Joshua did trust God, perhaps he was scared. Perhaps there are

times when you want God to help you and it takes a long time. Maybe you've started at a new school, or you've just moved house. It's important to remember that God always keeps his promises, and, as he said to Joshua, 'I will never leave you or forsake you. The Lord your God will be with you wherever you go.'

Song

Be bold, be strong (KS: 17)

Talk outline

 God wants us to be strong and brave when we start new things. It might be a new term, a new house, or a new year, but God is with us, just like he was with Joshua.

Song

Father, I place into your hands (KS2: 457)

Prayers

Ask God to help us to trust him better as we start new things.

You could base your prayers on the intercessions on page 31 of *Worship through the Christian Year: Year A*, adapted from *101 Ideas for Creative Prayer*.

Final hymn

Lord, for the years (SOF 2: 892)

Launchpad song plays as the congregation leaves.

Joshua

 Cast

Bertie Brainbox *(dressed in bow-tie, big glasses and white lab coat)*

Billy Beefcake *(well-built, but a bit stupid)*
  (Bertie and Billy are both played by adults pretending to be children.)

Old man

Moses *(in biblical costume)*

Caleb and other spies *(in biblical costumes)*

Joshua *(in tuxedo and bow-tie)*

God *(either off-stage voice or actor in balcony, pulpit or similar)*

 Props

Time machine

Football

Walking-stick

Smoke machine *(optional)*

Pen

Huge grapes *(use papier mâché)*

Sword

 Sound effects

Theme music (perhaps 'Back in Time' by Huey Lewis and the News) *(optional)*

Time machine

Theme music. Enter Billy Beefcake with football.

BILLY:	Bertie Brainbox! Are you here?
BERTIE:	*(Emerging from behind time machine)* Hello, Billy!
BILLY:	Are you playing football?
BERTIE:	I don't play football. I'm an inventor. I might injure my wonderful brain heading the ball. You know that, Billy Beefcake!
BILLY:	I forgot! What's this you're making?
BERTIE:	It's a time machine.
BILLY:	*(Looks blank)* What's that, then?
BERTIE:	Well, it's a device that allows one to travel back through a flaw in the time–space vortex to a parallel universe in which a modicum of integration is allowed into the historical timeframe.
BILLY:	Oh… *(Mystified)* What does that mean?
BERTIE:	You are a silly Billy! It means we can travel in time. Go back into the past and forward into the future.
BILLY:	*(Interested)* Oh! Could I go and say hello to my grandad?
BERTIE:	By jove, I think you've understood it. You could use the time machine to meet your grandad, say hello and have a cup of tea.
BILLY:	*(Confused)* I don't need to use the time machine to do that. He's just there. *(Waves at old man tottering past with walking-stick)* Hello, Grandad!

Reproduced with permission from *Launchpad* published by BRF 2004 (1 84101 326 9)

OLD MAN:	*(Waves)* Hello, Billy!
BERTIE:	You are a silly Billy! I meant you could meet your grandad as a little boy!
BILLY::	Oh! You mean travel back through a flaw in the time–space vortex to a parallel universe in which a modicum of integration is allowed into the historical timeframe?
BERTIE:	*(Open-mouthed)* Yes. That's it!
BILLY:	Well, why didn't you say so? How do you do it?
BERTIE:	You strap yourself in, and you set the switch here to the year you want, and then you press this button. *(Points to button)*
BILLY:	Oh. *(Presses it)* This button?

Smoke billows around time machine. FX signify take-off.

BERTIE:	Billy! You've pressed the switch!
BILLY:	I know!
BERTIE:	Now we're travelling in time!
BILLY:	I know!
BERTIE:	You are a silly Billy! I haven't finished building it yet! We could end up anywhere!

BILLY:	I'm sorry, Bertie! I'm a real silly Billy!
BERTIE:	*(Flicks switches frantically)* Yes, you are! I can't get it to stop. *(FX finish. Time machine has arrived)* Let's see what year it is.

Bertie cautiously opens door and creeps outside time machine. Enter Moses, Joshua, Caleb and other spies. Moses is briefing the others. Billy and Bertie crouch down.

MOSES:	God promised to give us this land of Canaan. He wants me to send spies to see what it's like. That's why I've called you—one spy from each tribe of Israel.
BILLY:	*(Pops his head up)* Bertie! Why are they all wearing dresses? Are we in heaven?
BERTIE:	I think we've gone back to the Old Testament. This is Moses, and these are the spies he's sending into Canaan! Keep out of the way, Billy. We don't want to interfere with history.
MOSES:	*(To Joshua)* Who are you? Are you a spy?
JOSHUA:	*(In Sean Connery voice)* The name's Joshua. Joshua Bond. This is my colleague Caleb. 007… 4521 is his phone number. OK, M. What's our mission?
MOSES:	Spy on Canaan. See how their crops grow and what the people are like.
JOSHUA:	OK, M. You got it. *(Takes out pen)* Shall I take this pen with me? It transforms into a speedboat at the flick of a switch.
MOSES:	*(Grabs pen)* No, Joshua. Just take God.
JOSHUA:	*(Normal voice)* Oh, OK.
BERTIE:	If I remember correctly, the spies went all over Canaan. *(Joshua, Caleb and other spies fan out

Reproduced with permission from *Launchpad* published by BRF 2004 (1 84101 326 9)

	across congregation, looking at everyone, particularly tall people) They spent forty days spying on the land.
BILLY:	Wow! Weren't they scared?
BERTIE:	Yes! Some of the spies were scared of the people they found. They looked very tall and strong. Some of them looked like giants!
OTHER SPIES:	*(Run around frantically, screaming)* Aaarrgghh!! Giants!!
BILLY:	*(Joining in)* Aaarrgghh! Giants!!
BERTIE:	*(Pulls him down, as Moses looks to see what the noise is)* No, Billy! They just thought they looked like giants!
BILLY:	Oh!
BERTIE:	The spies also found big, juicy grapes and other fruit, which showed that it would be a good land to live in.

Joshua and Caleb carry huge grapes back to Moses.

MOSES:	Wow! Look at the size of those grapes!
JOSHUA:	Yes, M. This is a good land!
CALEB:	Let's go there now. We know God will help us!
SPY 1:	M! We saw the people living there! They were huge! They looked like... giants!
OTHER SPIES:	*(Run round, screaming)* Aaarrgghh! Giants!
BILLY:	*(Runs around, screaming)* Aaarrgghh! Giants! *(Pulled down by Bertie)*
SPY 2:	We can't attack them. They're stronger than us. They'll step on us as if we were little grasshoppers! As if they were... giants!
OTHER SPIES:	*(Run around, screaming)* Aaarrgghh! Giants!
BILLY:	*(Runs around, screaming)* Aaarrgghh! Giants! *(Pulled down by Bertie)*

JOSHUA:	*(Points at congregation)* They're not giants. They're just normal people. We're not afraid of them, M. God is with us.
MOSES:	*(To other spies)* Please, let's go and fight the Canaanites. God will be with us. They're not giants!
OTHER SPIES:	*(Exit screaming. One drops sword)* Aaarrgghh! Giants!

BILLY:	*(Distressed)* Bertie! Where are the giants?
BERTIE:	There aren't any, you silly Billy!
MOSES:	*(To Joshua and Caleb)* Thank you for your work. I'll report back to God. *(They shake hands)*
CALEB:	*(To Joshua, as they exit)* How are you feeling, Joshua?
JOSHUA:	*(In Sean Connery voice again)* A little shaken, but not stirred... *(Exit)*
GOD:	Why won't my people trust me, Moses? Didn't I rescue them from Egypt? Didn't I help them find food and water in the desert? They don't deserve a new land full of good things.

MOSES:	We don't deserve it, Lord. But please give us a second chance.
GOD:	Not the grown-ups, because they wouldn't trust me. Just the children. They'll go in and enjoy the land—when they've grown up. Joshua and Caleb can too, because they trusted me. But not for another forty years. *(Exits)*
BILLY:	*(To Bertie)* Wow! They had to wait forty years before they were allowed into Canaan.
BERTIE:	That's right, Billy! And by that time, Moses had died.

Billy gets up, forgetting Moses is still there. Bertie tries to stop him, but is too late.

BILLY:	What did Moses die of, then, Bertie? *(Picks up sword)*
MOSES:	*(Catches sight of Billy brandishing sword)* Aaarrgghh! A giant!! *(Clutches chest and falls)*

Enter other spies, running around frantically.

OTHER SPIES:	*(Pointing at Billy)* Aaarrgghh! A giant!!
BERTIE:	You silly Billy! Let's get out of here!
BILLY:	*(Looking at Moses)* Oh no! I think he's dead!

Moses opens eyes, sees Billy and screams.

BILLY:	No, he isn't!

Bertie pulls Billy into time machine and fiddles with buttons.

BILLY:	Bertie! Have I messed everything up?
BERTIE:	*(Adjusting switches)* I don't know. We'll have to travel further in the Old Testament and see whether we've affected history. At least there's one thing we know.
BILLY:	What's that?
BERTIE:	Whatever we've done, God made a promise. And he will keep it.
BILLY:	Will he? So they will get to Canaan?
BERTIE:	Yes, Billy. We can trust God on that one.
BILLY:	Wow!
BERTIE:	It is rather exciting, isn't it, Billy, to see God's heroes in action?
BILLY:	Was Joshua one of God's heroes?
BERTIE:	Yes, Billy, because he trusted God.
BILLY:	Maybe we should visit more of God's heroes in your time machine—to see if God kept his promises to them.
BERTIE:	OK, Billy. I'll set a course through the Old Testament.

Theme music to end.

Reproduced with permission from *Launchpad* published by BRF 2004 (1 84101 326 9)

Samuel, the obedient boy

 Teaching point

We should listen to God and obey his instructions.

 Bible passages

1 Samuel 3:1–18; James 1:22–25.

 Key verse

God will bless you in everything you do, if you listen and obey, and don't just hear and forget.

JAMES 1:25

 Visual aids

OHP

The word 'prophet' written on an OHP acetate

Plain acetates or flipchart

Blindfold

SERVICE FRAMEWORK

★★★★★★★★★★★★★★★★★★★★★★★★★★★★★★★
★ ★
★ **Welcome the congregation.** ★
★ ★
★★★★★★★★★★★★★★★★★★★★★★★★★★★★★★★

Song

Sing the *Launchpad* song.

Talk outline

 Recap story of Billy and Bertie meeting Joshua.

Drama

God's heroes 2: Samuel *(see pages 22–25 for script)*.

Alternatively, read 'Samuel in the temple' from *Telling Even More Tales*, or read 'A Tale of Two Kings' in *50 Stories for Special Occasions*, and adjust talks as necessary.

Talk outline

 Who was the boy that Billy and Bertie met? Who kept calling him? Who did Samuel think it was? Sometimes we're not very good at listening to God. We're going to say sorry for that.

Confession

Father God, we're sorry that we sometimes hear what you say to us, but don't do anything about it. Please forgive us and help us to listen and obey. Amen.

Song

Come on and celebrate (KS: 34)

Activity

 Pick a child and blindfold them. Ask several people to call the child's name, including one of their parents, to see if the child can identify them. Say, 'Did you recognize any of those people? One of them was your mum/dad. Did you realize? Sometimes it's hard to recognize people just by their voices.'

Talk outline

Billy and Bertie met someone who didn't know who was calling him. Samuel was a special boy because his mum, Hannah, had asked God for a son. So when Samuel was born, Hannah promised that she would send him to work in the temple. Hannah kept her promise.

What was the priest's name? God wanted Samuel to pass on a message to Eli. In fact, God kept using Samuel as his messenger. That's why we call him a 'prophet' (show the word on OHP screen). God spoke to Samuel in a special way and the Bible tells us that God wants to speak to us too.

Activity

Ask the children how God speaks to us today. Write their answers on a flipchart or OHP acetate.

Talk outline

All of us have heard God in different ways. That's fine, because he knows how we work and what we listen to best. We might have thought that God would speak to Eli, because he was older and would know how to listen, but God didn't do that. He wanted Samuel, a small boy, to pass the message on.

Song

Prayer is like a telephone (KS: 286)

Activity

Ask for two child volunteers and blindfold one. While they are blindfolded, team members crouch in the aisle or put furniture in the way. The second child shouts instructions to the first one how

to get across the church. After the blindfolded child has completed the task, explain that the first child thought they knew the way, but they didn't know about the obstacles. They needed someone to guide them. When we hear God's instructions, we should listen, as he knows the way best.

Talk outline

Sometimes we're not sure if what we are hearing is God speaking, so it's important to check. The Bible is his special book to help us and that's the best place to look. So remember:

- God speaks to all of us.
- We need to listen and obey.
- We should check with the Bible.

Our reading tells us what to do when God speaks.

Reading

Read James 1:22–25.

Song

Speak Lord (KS: 307)

Prayers

Ask God to help us to listen and obey.

Final hymn

O Jesus, I have promised (SOF: 418)

Launchpad song plays as congregation leaves.

Samuel

 Cast

Bertie Brainbox
Billy Beefcake
Samuel *(played by a child in pyjamas)*
Eli *(old man in biblical costume)*
God *(either off-stage voice or actor in balcony, pulpit or similar)*

 Props

Time machine
Duvet
Slippers
Dressing-gown
Smoke machine *(optional)*
Torch
Sword
Fake blood *(optional)*

 Sound effects

Theme music *(optional)*
Time machine

Play theme music. Bertie and Billy enter time machine. Samuel lies under duvet and Eli sits in front of altar. Bertie fiddles with buttons.

BILLY: I'm glad you built this time machine, Bertie Brainbox! We had a dead good adventure when we saw Joshua! Where are we going next?

BERTIE: It's terribly exciting, Billy! Where would you like to go? Back in time to the Battle of Hastings, or to see the Romans? Or back to last Tuesday?

BILLY: Last Tuesday?

BERTIE: That was when I had stew and dumplings and jam roly-poly and custard. That's my favourite!

BILLY: *(Thinks deeply)* I'd like to see another one of God's heroes!

BERTIE: Of course! I am a silly Bertie! We were going to see more of God's heroes. I'll set this dial. Now, press the button and we'll travel back in time!

BILLY: *(Presses button. FX signify take-off. Smoke billows behind time machine)* This is dead exciting! Who do you think we'll meet this time?

BERTIE: I've set it for mid-Old Testament. Just after Joshua.

FX end. Bertie and Billy cautiously exit time machine.

BILLY: *(Feeling his way)* It's very dark, Bertie!

BERTIE: You are a silly Billy! That's because it's night-time!

BILLY: Oh! *(Falls over Samuel)* What's this, Bertie?

BERTIE:	I don't know! *(Gets out torch and switches it on, shining it on church walls and / or altar)* Look—we're in a temple!
BILLY:	A what?
BERTIE:	A tabernacle?
BILLY:	What?
BERTIE:	A place of worship! For the Israelites! This is where they met God.

BILLY:	Oh! *(Thinks deeply)* Bertie—isn't God everywhere?
BERTIE:	Yes… but this was their special place for meeting him.
BILLY:	Oh. So who's asleep on the floor?
GOD:	Samuel!
BILLY:	*(To Bertie)* You said that without moving your lips!
BERTIE:	You are a silly Billy! That wasn't me! It was… *(Looks up, then turns to Billy in amazement)* I think it was God!
GOD:	Samuel!
BILLY:	He's done it again! Do you think this is Samuel? Should I wake him up?

BERTIE:	Best not interfere, Billy. We don't want to distort the flaw in the time–space vortex to a parallel universe in which a modicum of integration is allowed into the historical timeframe.
GOD:	*(Louder)* Samuel! *(Samuel stirs)*
BERTIE:	Get out of the way! He's waking up!

Bertie and Billy hide. Samuel wakes up, puts on dressing-gown and slippers, and wanders over to Eli.

BILLY:	Who's that?
SAMUEL:	Eli?
BILLY:	*(To Bertie)* You said that without moving your lips as well!
ELI:	Yes?
SAMUEL:	You called, so here I am!
ELI:	*(Surprised)* I didn't call you, son. Go back to sleep!

Samuel goes back, takes off dressing-gown and slippers and gets back under duvet.

BILLY:	What happened?
BERTIE:	This old man, Eli, must be a priest, and is Samuel's boss. Samuel thinks Eli is calling his name, but it's God.
BILLY:	He's a bit of a silly Billy, then.
GOD:	Samuel!

Samuel gets up, puts on dressing-gown and slippers and wanders over to Eli.

BILLY:	No! Samuel! It's not Eli calling! It's God!
SAMUEL:	*(Slightly fed up)* Eli?
ELI:	Yes?
SAMUEL:	You called, so here I am!
BILLY:	No! It was God! Tell him, Bertie!
ELI:	I didn't call you, son. Go back to sleep!

Reproduced with permission from *Launchpad* published by BRF 2004 (1 84101 326 9)

Samuel goes back, takes off dressing-gown and slippers and gets back under duvet.

BILLY:	What shall we do? Samuel's not listening to God!
BERTIE:	It is a conundrum, isn't it? Shall we ask the people here to help? *(Points at congregation)*
BILLY:	Yeah! *(Approaches them)* Next time God calls Samuel, let's tell him it's God. OK? Shout out: 'Samuel! It's God speaking!' Ready? *(They hide again)*
GOD:	Samuel!
BILLY/BERTIE/	
CONGREGATION:	Samuel! It's God speaking!

Samuel gets up, puts on dressing-gown and slippers and wanders over to Eli.

SAMUEL:	*(More fed up)* Eli?
ELI:	Yes?
SAMUEL:	You called, so here I am!
ELI:	*(Pauses)* Samuel. It's not me calling. Maybe it's God. Next time you hear a voice, say, 'Speak, Lord, for your servant is listening!'
BILLY:	Hooray! Eli told him!

Samuel goes back, takes off dressing-gown and slippers and gets back under duvet.

BERTIE:	I wonder what God will say to him!
GOD:	Samuel!
SAMUEL:	*(Sits up)* Speak, Lord, for your servant is listening!
GOD:	Samuel, I have some bad news. Eli's sons have done some bad things, and he didn't stop them. Therefore I'll have to punish his whole family. You must tell him.
SAMUEL:	I understand, Lord.

Samuel goes to sleep again. Billy and Bertie emerge from hiding.

BERTIE:	Billy! It isn't good news. I wonder if he'll tell Eli!
BILLY:	*(Gets out sword)* If Eli's sons have done something bad, I'll punish them!
BERTIE:	*(Restrains him)* No, Billy! That's God's business!
BILLY:	*(Pushes him off and wields sword)* No, I can do it!

Billy pretends he's slicing someone in two—and hits Bertie.

BERTIE:	*(Holding arm—fake blood could be used)* Aaarrgghh! Billy! You've hit me!
BILLY:	I didn't mean to!
BERTIE:	You are a silly Billy! I'm bleeding!
BILLY:	Let's get you to hospital!
BERTIE:	There are no hospitals in the Old Testament! And I can't work the time machine because I'm hurt. You're going to have to work the time machine to get us… *(pointing dramatically into congregation)* back to the future!

Reproduced with permission from *Launchpad* published by BRF 2004 (1 84101 326 9)

BILLY:	I'm no good at working time machines!
BERTIE:	It's OK! I'll tell you what to do!

Billy helps Bertie to his feet and into time machine. Samuel nervously gets up.

BERTIE:	Look! Let's see if Samuel tells Eli the bad news.
ELI:	Samuel! What did God say to you?
SAMUEL:	He said your sons did some bad things, and you didn't stop them. Therefore he will punish your whole family.

Eli hangs his head, but puts his hand on Samuel's shoulder.

BILLY:	He said it, Bertie! He obeyed God!
BERTIE:	*(With a flash of inspiration)* Of course, Billy! This small boy will grow up to be the prophet Samuel!
BILLY:	He doesn't look like a prophet to me!
BERTIE:	Don't you see? Because he listened to God and obeyed him as a boy, God used him as a messenger when he was grown up! It's all in the Bible!

Eli and Samuel exit.

BILLY:	So, what do I do to operate this, then?
BERTIE:	You really need a GCSE in advanced time travel… *(Billy's face falls)* Ah. We haven't got time for that. If you listen to what I say and do everything I tell you, we should be fine.
BILLY:	OK.
BERTIE:	First, you need to adjust the visual information locators for the parallel timeframe.
BILLY:	*(Stares)* What?

BERTIE:	Set the date and time dials for… *(insert today's date).*
BILLY:	Oh. *(Does so)* Done that.
BERTIE:	Now you need to fix the personnel anti-ejector straps.
BILLY:	What?
BERTIE:	Fasten the seatbelts!
BILLY:	Oh. *(Does so)* Done that!
BERTIE:	Now you need to fire the retro-thrust capacitors which will boost us into the flaw in the time–space continuum!
BILLY:	What?
BERTIE:	Press that button!
BILLY:	Oh. *(Does so. FX signify take-off)* I've done that as well! Bertie! I've helped us take off!
BERTIE:	Well done, Billy! That was really good!
BILLY:	Do you know what I did? I listened to you and obeyed your instructions, just like Samuel did with God!
BERTIE:	So you did! I do believe we've learnt something else on our travels, Billy. I wonder where we'll end up next!

Theme music to end.

Reproduced with permission from *Launchpad* published by BRF 2004 (1 84101 326 9)

Esther, the courageous queen

 Teaching point
Be brave and do the right thing.

 Bible passages
Esther 2:19—7:10; Luke 10:30–35.

 Key verse
Dear friends, you must never become tired of doing right.
2 THESSALONIANS 3:13

 Visual aids
For *Egg Walk* (if used):
Blindfold
Six hard-boiled eggs
Cornflakes or similar breakfast cereal
Newspaper
Dustpan and brush
Two small creme eggs

SERVICE FRAMEWORK

★★★★★★★★★★★★★★★★★★★★★★★★★★★★
★ ★
★ **Welcome the congregation.** ★
★ ★
★★★★★★★★★★★★★★★★★★★★★★★★★★★★

Song

Sing the *Launchpad* song.

Talk outline

 Recap the story of Billy and Bertie meeting Samuel.

Drama

God's heroes 3: Esther *(see pages 28–31 for script)*.

Alternatively, read 'Queen Esther' from *Telling Even More Tales*.

Talk outline

 Recap on the story, emphasizing that Esther was one of God's people and that she had to be brave to save them from Haman. Why was that brave? Esther knew the right thing to do, and did it. Billy and Bertie weren't as brave as Esther. Would you be as brave? Sometimes it is frightening to do the right thing.

Song

Do you know what is right? (KS 2: 448)

Confession

Father God, we don't always do the right thing. We don't always do what you ask us to do. Please forgive us for those times when we let you down. Amen.

Song

I'm special (KS: 162)

Activity

 Ask four children to act out some playground situations.

1. Three children all have the latest must-have toy *(give an example)*. The fourth doesn't, and is sad. Two of them laugh at him/her because he/she hasn't got it. What should the third child do? *(Share the toy.)*

2. One child is being bullied by two bigger children. A fourth child sees it happening. What should you do if you see this happening? *(Tell a teacher.)*

3. One child throws stones at a window. Two others join in. They want the fourth to join in as well. What should the fourth do? *(Don't join in—go home.)*

Alternative activity

 Ask children to do the 'Egg Walk' on page 16 of *The Road to Easter*.

Reading

Read Luke 10:30–35.

Talk outline

 The Samaritan did the right thing. Was he brave? Why? We don't usually help our enemies. We normally help our friends. But Jesus asks us to love our enemies too.

Optional story

'The Making of a Hero' from *50 Stories for Special Occasions*.

Song

Shake a friend's hand (KS: 293)

Prayers

Ask God to help us to be brave and do the right thing.

Final hymn

Be thou my vision (SOF: 42)

Launchpad song plays as the congregation leaves.

Esther

 Cast

Bertie Brainbox
Billy Beefcake
King Xerxes *(in biblical costume)*
Guards *(in biblical costume)*
Haman *(in biblical costume)*
Esther *(in biblical costume)*
Mordecai *(in biblical costume)*

 Props

Time machine
Smoke machine *(optional)*
Throne
Sword
Scroll
Golden sceptre *(perhaps a churchwarden's stave)*

 Sound effects

Theme music
Time machine

Play theme music. Bertie and Billy enter time machine. Xerxes sits on throne.

BILLY:	I'm so excited, Bertie Brainbox! Your brilliant time machine has taken us to see two of God's best heroes! Where will we end up next?
BERTIE:	I don't know, Billy Beefcake. I've set the machine for later in the Old Testament. But I'm not sure we really want to go.
BILLY:	Why not?
BERTIE:	It was a terribly difficult time for God's people. They'd been taken prisoner and had to live in another country.
BILLY:	Oh. Maybe I could tell some jokes?
BERTIE:	They don't need jokes! They want a hero to stand up for them! Let's see if they find one. Press the button, Billy.
BILLY:	*(FX signify take-off)* I think I'm getting used to this!
BERTIE:	We should land near the king's palace. *(FX stop)* Let's see where we are! *(They exit time machine and see Xerxes on his throne)* Who's that? He looks important!
BILLY:	*(Approaches Xerxes and offers hand)* Hello! Who are you?
XERXES:	How dare you! I am the king! King Xerxes!
BILLY:	Oh. Hello!
XERXES:	*(Grabs Billy)* Do you know what happens to people who approach me without an invitation?
BILLY:	Er… no, I don't, your Majesty!

XERXES:	They get killed for their impertinence! *(Shouts)* Guards! Take this imbecile away!
BERTIE:	You are a silly Billy! You shouldn't have done that!
XERXES:	Aha! Another one! *(Grabs Bertie)* You will also die!
BILLY:	Bertie! What are we going to do? They'll kill us!

Guards enter and grab Billy and Bertie.

BERTIE:	I know! Into the time machine! *(Billy and Bertie break free and run into time machine)* Quick! Close the doors!
XERXES:	*(To guards)* After them!

Guards run over and hammer on time machine.

BILLY:	What are you going to do?
BERTIE:	I'm setting the dial for five minutes ago. That way, it'll be as if you'd never spoken to the king like that!

Bertie presses button. FX. Billy, Bertie, Xerxes and the guards repeat previous actions in reverse at high speed, as if a tape is rewinding. All deliver nonsense 'lines' as if speaking backwards at high speed. At the point where time machine landed, Billy and Bertie go forwards again.

BERTIE	We should land near the king's palace. *(FX stop)* Let's see where we are! *(They exit the time machine and see Xerxes sitting on his throne)* Who's that? He looks important. *(Billy approaches Xerxes, but Bertie stops him)* Billy! Don't do it again! Remember—if you approach him without an invitation, he'll kill you!
BILLY:	Oh yeah!

Billy and Bertie hide. Haman approaches Xerxes.

XERXES:	Haman, you are honoured before all other nobles. I welcome you to my palace!

Xerxes waves golden sceptre to signify that Haman can speak.

HAMAN:	*(Bows)* Thank you, your Majesty. I have news. There are some people called the Israelites who don't obey your laws. If it pleases you, I would like to kill them all.
BERTIE:	The Israelites are God's people! He wants to kill them!
BILLY:	I won't let him…! *(Emerges with sword. Bertie restrains him)*
BERTIE:	No, Billy!
XERXES:	You have my permission.
HAMAN:	*(Bows low)* Thank you, your Majesty.

Haman exits.

BILLY:	We can't let him kill the Israelites! Let's tell the king they are God's people!

BERTIE:	*(Wrestling with conscience)* I say, Billy, it's a tricky situation. But you heard the king. If we approach him without being asked, he will kill us! I'm not going through that again!
BILLY:	You can't let God's people die, Bertie! You know that's not right.
BERTIE:	Let's see if there's another way to help! Come on, let's sneak out of here!

They drop to the floor and crawl away from Xerxes. Enter Esther and Mordecai.

ESTHER:	But, Mordecai, what can I do?
MORDECAI:	You're an Israelite, Esther! Don't you want to save your people?
ESTHER:	Of course!
MORDECAI:	And you're married to the king!
BILLY:	*(Stands)* Bertie! She must be the queen! *(Bertie pulls him down)*
ESTHER:	I might be the queen, but if I approach the king without being asked, he'll kill me…
BERTIE:	*(Stands)* I say, Billy! He would even kill his wife if she approached him! *(Crouches down again)*

BILLY:	*(Stands)* Yeah. My dad's the same. Especially if he's watching football. He doesn't like Mum interrupting… *(Bertie pulls him down)*
ESTHER:	…unless the king waves his golden sceptre. That means it's OK.
MORDECAI:	Please, Esther, you must do something. That's why God made you queen! Quick! It's Haman!

Esther and Mordecai exit. Haman enters with scroll.

HAMAN:	Hear this, Israelites! On the 13th of next month, the king has said you'll all be killed—young and old, women and children. No one shall be spared.
BERTIE:	Does the king know his wife is an Israelite?
BILLY:	What's going to happen, Bertie?
BERTIE:	I don't know. But if Esther goes to talk to the king, then she's braver than me!

Enter Esther, approaching Xerxes.

BILLY:	Bertie! She's coming!
BERTIE:	I can't bear to look! Will he kill her as well?
ESTHER:	*(Bows low)* Your Majesty!
XERXES:	*(Thinks, then waves golden sceptre)* What is it, my lovely wife?
BILLY:	Phew! He didn't kill her!
ESTHER:	I need to tell you something, your Majesty. I'm an Israelite, and someone is trying to have us all killed.
XERXES:	Who is this vile person?
ESTHER:	*(Points at Haman)* It's him! Haman!
XERXES:	*(To Haman)* How dare you! This is my wife, and these are her people!

HAMAN:	A thousand apologies, your Majesty! I had no idea!
XERXES:	I don't want any of them killed. But I am going to kill you! Guards! Take him away!

Enter guards.

HAMAN:	*(As guards drag him off)* No! No!
BILLY:	*(Stands)* Hooray! Well done, Esther!
XERXES:	I will give all Haman's land to you and Mordecai, Esther. The Israelites can do what they like.
BERTIE:	*(Stands)* This is a turn-up! Is this really what happened in the Bible?
XERXES:	*(Looks at Bertie and Billy)* Who is this, that dares to approach the king without being asked? Guards!

Bertie and Billy look at each other.

BERTIE:	Quick! Into the time machine again!

They run into time machine. Guards run on, but can't find Billy and Bertie.

BILLY:	Let's go somewhere else in the Old Testament, Bertie! Before they find us!
BERTIE:	*(Fiddling with dials)* I'm trying, Billy!

Xerxes waves guards away. They exit, as do Xerxes and Esther.

BILLY:	Esther was very brave, wasn't she? She decided to go and see the king, even though he might have killed her!
BERTIE:	That's right. She saved her people!
BILLY:	*(Looks down)* We weren't so brave, were we? We knew what might happen, but we were afraid, weren't we?
BERTIE:	Well, obviously, I would have spoken to the king, but it might have upset the flaw in the time–space vortex to a parallel universe in which a modicum of integration is allowed into the historical timeframe…
BILLY:	Really?
BERTIE:	Er… no. You're right. I was afraid too. We knew the right thing to do, but we didn't do it. Maybe we'll get on better when we meet God's next hero.

Theme music to end.

Jonah, the reluctant prophet

 Teaching point

God loves badly behaved people too.

 Bible passages

Jonah 3:1—4:11; Matthew 5:43–48

 Key verse

You are a kind and merciful God, and you are very patient. You always show love, and you don't like to punish anyone, not even foreigners.
JONAH 4:2

Visual aids

Photographs of famous people *(see activity below)*.

SERVICE FRAMEWORK

★ ★
★   ★
★   **Welcome the congregation.**   ★
★   ★
★ ★

Song

Sing the *Launchpad* song.

Talk outline

 Recap the story of Billy and Bertie meeting Esther.

Drama

God's heroes 4: Jonah *(see pages 34–37 for script)*.

Alternatively, read 'Jonah and the Whale' from *Telling Tales*.

Talk outline

 Recap on the story, emphasizing the fact that Jonah thought the people of Nineveh were God's enemies. What surprised him? They decided to become God's friends. How did God show him they were important? He gave Jonah a big plant. When it withered, Jonah was angry. But God said: 'That plant was important to you, and you were upset when it died. These people are more important than a plant, and I was upset when they weren't my friends.'

Sometimes we're not good at seeing things like God does. But God loves badly behaved people as well as those who behave in the way they should.

Confession

Father God, forgive us when we think we are better than people who don't follow you. Help us to see that you love everyone the same. Amen.

Song

What a whale of a tale (KS: 368).

Reading

Read Matthew 5:43–48

Song

Don't repay evil with evil (KS: 42)

Activity

 Display photos of famous people. Include those who might be considered to be on God's side (for example, your vicar / minister; Diana, Princess of Wales; a saint; or Mother Teresa), those who might be considered to be against God (such as a robber; the latest villain from EastEnders or Coronation Street; Saddam Hussein; Myra Hindley), and some that people might not be sure about (the Prime Minister; a sports star, a pop group). Ask which of the famous people are 'good' and which are 'bad'. Then ask which of them God loves. Finally, point out that all the people in the photographs have the potential to behave well or badly and that God loves them all.

Alternative activity

 Tell the story of Burglar Bill from page 122 of *Worship through the Christian Year: Year B*.

Talk outline

Whether we behave well or badly, God loves us and wants to help us. That's good news, because we all have the capacity to behave badly sometimes.

Song

Thank you for saving me (KS2: 713)

Prayers

Pray that God will help all people, however they behave, to discover his love.

Final hymn

Praise, my soul, the king of heaven (SOF: 466)

Launchpad song plays as the congregation leaves.

Jonah

 Cast

Bertie Brainbox
Billy Beefcake
Ninevites *(in biblical costume)*
Jonah *(behaves like a spoilt teenager)*
God *(offstage voice or actor in balcony, pulpit or similar)*

 Props

Time machine
Empty cans of beer
Unlit cigarettes
Smoke machine *(optional)*
Real plant or paper plant that can 'wither'

 Sound effects

Theme music
Time machine

Play theme music. Bertie and Billy enter time machine. Enter Ninevites with beer and cigarettes.

BERTIE: That was close, Billy! We just got out of King Xerxes' palace in time. This time-travelling is dangerous!

BILLY: I enjoy it, Bertie. I liked Queen Esther and the brave way she saved God's people.

BERTIE: I've set the dial for later in the Old Testament. Do you want to press the button?

BILLY: Yes please! *(He does. FX start)* Will we meet more of God's people?

BERTIE: We might, Billy! Hang on… we're going off course! *(Frantically adjusts dials)*

BILLY: *(Frightened)* Where are we going?

BERTIE: Into Assyria! The people there were the enemies of the Israelites. There won't be any of God's people there.

BILLY: *(Grabs hold of Bertie tightly)* Bertie, I'm frightened!

BERTIE: *(Muffled)* Hhmmghhh!

BILLY: What's that, Bertie?

BERTIE: *(Muffled)* Hhmmghhh!!

BILLY: *(Confused)* I·can't hear you! *(Puts ear to Bertie's mouth and lets go)*

BERTIE: *(Loudly)* I said, 'You've got your hand over my mouth!'

BILLY: *(Looks in confusion at his hand and Bertie's mouth)* No, I haven't! You are a silly Bertie! And you're supposed to be clever! *(Turns and exits time machine)* Let's see where we

Reproduced with permission from *Launchpad* published by BRF 2004 (1 84101 326 9)

	are! *(Ninevites start fighting, smoking and drinking. Billy turns back)* Bertie, they don't look very nice.
NINEVITE 1:	*(Aggressively, drinking beer)* Whadda yer want, stupid?
BERTIE:	Excuse me, my good man. Is this Nineveh?
NINEVITE 2:	*(Spits)* What's it to you?
BERTIE:	Goodness me, Billy! I don't think these are God's people!
BILLY:	It's just like being at *(insert local football ground)*!
NINEVITE 1:	This is Nineveh. We don't believe in any god. And you're not welcome. Why don't you clear off?
BERTIE:	We might just do that! We don't like it here! *(Ninevites return to their bad behaviour)* Let's go, Billy! We want to find God's heroes. There are certainly none here.
BILLY:	Hold on, Bertie! Who's that?

Enter Jonah, dripping wet.

BERTIE:	Goodness me! He looks soaking, Billy! *(Approaches Jonah)* What happened?
JONAH:	It's so unfair! I spent three days in a whale's belly. That's why I'm wet.
BILLY:	Ah! We once spent three days in Wales. It rained every day and we got soaked. We go to the Isle of Wight for our holidays now.
JONAH:	*(Incredulously)* Huh? No, three days inside a whale! Just because I was running away from God. It's so unfair!
BERTIE:	Ah! So you're one of God's people. But you shouldn't run away from God!
JONAH:	He told me to come here and tell people to stop behaving badly or he'd punish them. I didn't want to come.

BILLY:	*(Smells the air)* Bertie, I can smell fish. *(Looks for fish. To Jonah)* Can you smell it?
BERTIE:	That's a terribly difficult thing to ask. These people look really awful!

JONAH:	I went in this boat, and there was a storm. The sailors thought it would sink. They blamed me because I was running away from God, so they threw me in the sea. And I was swallowed by this whale. I only got out of the whale's belly because it was sick on the beach!
BILLY:	I was sick when I came out of Wales as well. Maybe the Severn Bridge was too wobbly… *(Bertie cuffs him)*
BERTIE:	You are a silly Billy! This is Jonah, and he's supposed to be preaching to the people of Nineveh!
BILLY:	*(Pulls Bertie to one side)* Is he one of God's heroes, then?

Reproduced with permission from *Launchpad* published by BRF 2004 (1 84101 326 9)

BERTIE:	I think so. But he doesn't look like one.
BILLY:	Neither did Joshua or Samuel or Esther! Remember—we learnt that God chooses people you don't expect.
JONAH:	*(Gets out a scroll and reads half-heartedly to Ninevites)* 'People of Nineveh! God says he will destroy your city in forty days because of your wickedness!' *(Turns his back on them)* Done it! Can I go home now?
NINEVITE 1:	He's right! We are wicked! We should change!
NINEVITE 2:	Let's fast and pray to God and ask if he will save us!
NINEVITE 1:	Let's start being nicer to each other!
NINEVITE 2:	Yes, God might have pity on us and not destroy the city!

They discard drinks, stub out cigarettes and kneel, pleading for mercy.

BERTIE:	That was very effective preaching! How did he do that?
BILLY:	God must have helped!
JONAH:	But God said he will definitely destroy the city of Nineveh. There's no point in them praying.
BILLY:	But they've changed! They're not being evil any more!
JONAH:	They've got no chance. Once God decides something, that's it. *(To Ninevites)* You can stop that. It won't work!
GOD:	Jonah! This is God. I'm not going to destroy Nineveh after all.
JONAH:	Huh? Why not?
GOD:	Because I'm kind and merciful, and very patient. I always show love, and don't like to punish anyone, not even…
JONAH:	*(Recites it with him)* …not even foreigners. Yes, I know! Huh! You didn't really need me to come and preach at all. I could have stayed at home and you could have forgiven them anyway. It's so unfair! *(Sits in a sulk)* I just want to sit here and die!
BERTIE:	But, Jonah, this is the terribly complicated thing about God.

Reproduced with permission from *Launchpad* published by BRF 2004 (1 84101 326 9)

	He *could* have done it by himself, but he chooses to use people like you as heroes. Even though you're not very heroic.
BILLY:	I can still smell fish, Bertie? Is it you?
BERTIE:	No, Billy—it's Jonah! It's whales you can smell!
BILLY:	Don't be silly, Bertie! We're thousands of miles from Wales!
JONAH:	It's so hot sitting here! It's *so* unfair!
GOD:	OK, Jonah. Here's something to keep you in the shade. *(Indicates plant)*
JONAH:	Right. I suppose I can use that to keep out of the sun. *(Sits under it)*
BILLY:	He doesn't seem very happy, Bertie. Maybe it's all that time he spent in Wales.
BERTIE:	He's got a bit of an attitude. Maybe God's sorting him out. *(Plant withers)*
JONAH:	Huh! It's so unfair! I hate this plant! It was keeping me in the shade, and now it's died. It's so hot. I feel faint.
GOD:	Are you angry about the plant, Jonah?
JONAH:	Too right!
GOD:	You're really bothered about that plant, though you didn't grow or feed or water it. It sprang up overnight and died overnight. But Nineveh has lots of people. Shouldn't you be more bothered about their lives than this plant?
JONAH:	Huh! It's so unfair! Why are you always right about everything? Yes, I should be concerned about these people… *(Goes to talk to Ninevites)*
BILLY:	Is that right, Bertie? Should Jonah help them, even though they were behaving badly?
BERTIE:	That's right, Billy. God loves

people even when they behave badly—because he wants to forgive them and help them start again. He sent Jonah to Nineveh, even though they were God's enemies.

BILLY:	*(As they re-enter time machine)* Wow! So God wasn't just concerned about the Israelites?
BERTIE:	That's right, Billy. You're learning very quickly. Maybe you're not such a silly Billy after all!
BILLY:	*(Proudly)* Thank you, Bertie! I've just got one more question.
BERTIE:	Fire away!
BILLY:	What about the people of Wales? What have they got to do with it?
BERTIE:	*(Despairingly)* You are such a silly Billy! Let's go and meet some more of God's heroes. And do stop going on about Wales!

Theme music to end.

Reproduced with permission from *Launchpad* published by BRF 2004 (1 84101 326 9)

John the Baptist: Follow Jesus!

 Teaching point

Follow Jesus!

 Bible passage

Mark 1:1–18.

 Key verse

'Turn back to God and be baptized. Then your sins will be forgiven.'

MARK 1:4

 Visual aids

Simple costumes to denote Bible heroes or Christian heroes, or photographs / illustrations of them *(see activity below)*.

Photographs of members of the congregation.

Stickers with the words 'I'm one of God's heroes' written on them *(see template on page 39 or download from www.launchpad-services.com)*.

SERVICE FRAMEWORK

★★★★★★★★★★★★★★★★★★★★★★★★★★★★★
★   ★
★   **Welcome the congregation.**   ★
★   ★
★★★★★★★★★★★★★★★★★★★★★★★★★★★★★

Song

Sing the *Launchpad* song.

Talk outline

 Recap the story of Billy and Bertie meeting Jonah.

Activity

 Dress children as Bible heroes (including some whom Billy and Bertie have met) or Christian heroes such as Martin Luther, William Wilberforce or Mother Teresa, or show pictures of them, and ask what made them heroic.

Drama

God's heroes 5: John the Baptist (part one) *(see pages 40–44 for script)*.

Song

Jesus is greater than the greatest heroes (KS: 196)

Talk outline

 Recap the story, emphasizing the fact that we don't need to have met Jesus in person to know him. Ask how we can follow Jesus today.

Activity

 Point out 'God's heroes' in the congregation (people who care for people when they are unwell, help run children's activities, or help with the running of the church). Put their photos alongside the heroes mentioned earlier.

Drama

God's heroes 5: John the Baptist (part two) *(see page 44 for script)*.

Prayers

Father God, thank you for the example of all your heroes, especially your son Jesus. We're sorry that we don't always follow his example. Help us to learn how to be your heroes too. Amen.

Final hymn

So I've made up my mind (that I'm gonna follow him) (KS: 301) or
I wanna be with you, Jesus (*The Big Book of Spring Harvest Kids' Praise*: 47)

Drama

God's heroes 5: John the Baptist (part three) *(see pages 44–45 for script)*.

Final song

We wanna see Jesus lifted high (KS: 365)

Launchpad song plays as congregation leaves. Billy and Bertie give out stickers saying 'I'm one of God's heroes' to the congregation as they go.

I'm one of God's heroes

John the Baptist

 Cast

Bertie Brainbox
Billy Beefcake
John the Baptist *(in shabby clothes)*
Crowd *(in biblical costumes)*

 Props

Time machine
Smoke machine *(optional)*
Placards saying 'Repent and be baptized' and 'The end of the world is nigh'
Partially filled paddling pool *(or use baptistry if available)*

 Sound effects

Theme music
Time machine
Loud crash

 Visual effects

Countdown from 10 to 1, then 'Blast Off'

PART ONE

Play theme music. Billy and Bertie enter time machine.

BILLY:	Phew, Bertie! I'm exhausted after meeting God's heroes!
BERTIE:	I say, Billy! It has been terribly exciting. There was Joshua, who trusted in God…
BILLY:	Samuel, who listened to God and obeyed him…
BERTIE:	Esther, who bravely did the right thing…
BILLY:	Jonah, who discovered that God loves people even when they behave badly…
BERTIE:	Do you know what we haven't done yet, Billy?
BILLY:	Er… *(Thinks)* I know! We haven't seen Adam and Eve with no clothes on… *(Giggles)*
BERTIE:	That's true…
BILLY:	We haven't seen where the animals go to the toilet on Noah's Ark! Or played eleven-a-side football with Joseph's brothers…!
BERTIE:	That's not what I meant! We haven't been in the New Testament. We haven't met God's biggest hero.
BILLY:	*(As though he understands)* Oh! *(In confusion)* Who's that, then?
BERTIE:	Jesus is the biggest of God's heroes in the Bible. He's terribly important, because he's God's son! I think we should go and see him when he was about thirty. *(Sets dials)*

BILLY:	OK! And I'll press the button! *(He does. FX)*
BERTIE:	Hold on, Billy! Oh, you've done it! I meant to say—we might have some turbulence!

Billy and Bertie flail around in time machine.

BILLY:	It's a very bumpy ride, Bertie!
BERTIE:	That's because we're going from BC to AD—from before Christ to after his birth. We've got to go through the Apocrypha into the New Testament. There's a big black hole between the end of Malachi and the beginning of Matthew's Gospel…

FX: big crash. Billy and Bertie fall over. Bertie emerges, his glasses askew. FX stop.

BERTIE:	Oh no, Billy! I think it's broken!

Bertie exits time machine and looks underneath.

BILLY:	Oh no! It's all my fault!
BERTIE:	There's a big leak in the fuel pipes. This is terrible! In another five minutes, we'll have no fuel left.
BILLY:	You mean, if we don't hurry, we won't be able to get *(points dramatically into congregation)* back to the future!
BERTIE:	That's right!
JOHN:	*(Offstage)* Repent, for the kingdom of heaven is near!
BILLY:	Perhaps this man can help.

Billy exits time machine. Enter John the Baptist, carrying placard saying, 'Repent and be baptized'. Crowd follows enthusiastically.

BILLY:	Excuse me! Have you any fuel?
JOHN:	Prepare ye the way of the Lord!
BILLY:	*(To Bertie)* What fuel do we need, Bertie?
BERTIE:	Ah. A mixture of depleted uranium molecules with a combination of diesel motor fuel and lead replacement nuclear-powered petrol.
BILLY:	*(Grabs Bertie)* Will they have that in Jesus' time?
BERTIE:	No.
BILLY:	Then we're doomed! *(Marches around, shouting frantically)* The end of the world is nigh! *(Grabs placard from crowd saying, 'The end of the world is nigh')* We're finished!
JOHN:	*(Shouting equally frantically, following Billy)* No, you're not finished! You have to repent and be baptized!
BILLY:	We're all going to die!
JOHN:	Yes, but you can enter the kingdom of heaven if you repent!
BERTIE:	*(Interrupting)* I say! You're not… John the Baptist, are you?
JOHN:	That's right! Do you want to be baptized?

Reproduced with permission from *Launchpad* published by BRF 2004 (1 84101 326 9)

BERTIE:	Not really…
JOHN:	Do you admit you've done wrong things?

John grabs Bertie and propels him to pool of water / baptistry.

BILLY:	Oh yes! He's done lots wrong! He just crashed our time machine so we can't get home!
BERTIE:	That's true…
JOHN:	Do you want to say sorry and make a new start with God? Because there is one coming after me who is more powerful than me, whose sandals I am not fit to carry!
BERTIE:	*(Gulps and looks around)* You mean… Jesus?
JOHN:	That's right! Do you want to follow him?
BERTIE:	Yes, I do!

JOHN:	*(Dunks Bertie's head underwater)* In that case… I baptize you and ask God to forgive you. *(Bertie is brought back to the surface)*
BILLY:	Ha ha! That was funny, Bertie!

JOHN:	*(To Billy)* What about you? How do you feel about God, Billy?
BILLY:	*(Gulps)* Well, I've got nothing against him…
JOHN:	Would you like to make a new start with God, and repent of those things you've done wrong? *(Grabs Billy)*
BILLY:	Yes! And I want to follow Jesus as well!
JOHN:	*(Dunks Billy's head underwater)* I baptize you and ask God to forgive you. *(To Bertie)* I baptize with water, but the one who comes after me will baptize you with the Holy Spirit. *(Billy struggles for air)* Jesus is the Messiah. *(Bertie tries to point out that Billy is struggling)* He is the Son of God. He's asking people to follow him and be his disciples.
BERTIE:	Excuse me, Mr the Baptist… *(John realizes and pulls Billy out of water)* Billy! Jesus is here!
BILLY:	Wow! I think I'd like to be one of his disciples!
BERTIE:	It would be terribly exciting, Billy, but we can't wait! *(Looks at watch)* We only have another thirty seconds before we run out of fuel completely. Either we go now, or we have to stay here for ever.
BILLY:	Oh no! My mum will be worried. She thinks I've gone out to play football before my tea.
BERTIE:	My dad thinks I'm messing about in the garage with my tool-kit.
BILLY:	But I'd really like to stay here and meet Jesus!
BERTIE:	We can't! Quick, let's go! Goodbye Mr the Baptist!

John exits. Billy and Bertie rush into time machine. FX: countdown starts.

BERTIE: We've only got ten seconds! *(Congregation join countdown as Bertie makes adjustments)* I've set it to *(insert today's date and name of church)*, Billy!

Countdown reaches zero as Bertie hits button. FX.

BILLY: Phew, that was close! We nearly didn't make it!

BERTIE: I hope we've got enough fuel to get us back to the present. *(FX: time machine starts petering out)* Look at this... it's 1990... 1995... 2000... 2002... *(insert correct year)*. *(FX: time machine grinds to a halt)* Phew! We only just made it. And now there's no fuel left. I think our time-travelling days are over, Billy!

BILLY: Oh no! Now we'll never meet Jesus. And we'll never meet any more of God's heroes.

BERTIE: Let's see where we are.

Bertie exits time machine and looks around.

BILLY: I'm really sad, Bertie, because I promised to follow Jesus, and I didn't even get to see him!

Billy exits time machine.

BERTIE: *(Suddenly aware of congregation)* Shh, Billy! We seem to be in the middle of a church service!

BILLY: *(Waves idiotically)* Hello! *(To Bertie)* Bertie, they seem to be watching us!

BERTIE: I know. Maybe if we just go and sit down, they won't notice.

They edge away from time machine, looking embarrassed.

BILLY: *(Thought suddenly strikes him)* But a time machine has just landed at the front of church— of course they'll notice! I wonder if any of them know anything about Jesus?

BERTIE: *(To children)* Terribly sorry about landing in the middle of your church! Have you been watching us? Do you know anything about Jesus? *(Allow child to respond)*

BILLY: *(Approaches service leader)* Excuse me. Do you know Jesus? Have you been back in a time machine to meet him?

LEADER: Yes, I know him, but I didn't have to go back in a time machine to become one of his followers.

BILLY: Didn't you? Bertie! I think I've found another one of God's heroes. But he's never met Jesus either!

BERTIE: It's terribly exciting! These children are God's heroes too! They know all about us—and the Bible!

BILLY: Gosh, Bertie! You don't think all

Reproduced with permission from *Launchpad* published by BRF 2004 (1 84101 326 9)

	these people are God's heroes, do you?
BERTIE:	*(Looks at congregation)* Don't be silly, Billy! Look at that one over there! *(Points out one person)* He looks a shady character!
BILLY:	But I don't think any of them have actually met Jesus in person, have they? *(To congregation)* Have any of you gone back in a time machine and met Jesus? *(No response)* But do you all know Jesus? *(Congregation responds)*
BERTIE:	Ah! But I bet none of you have been baptized and promised to follow him! *(Congregation responds)* Oh! Billy, I think we've found more of God's heroes.
BILLY:	That's really exciting, Bertie! I'm going to meet some of them now!

Billy delves into congregation. Bertie follows. They sit, talking to children.

| LEADER: | Well, perhaps we should be getting on with our service now… |

PART TWO

BILLY:	*(Interrupts service leader)* Excuse me, but we've already been baptized and promised to follow Jesus! Isn't that all we need to do?
LEADER:	You can do more than that. You can listen to what he says in the Bible and do it. And you can pray to him every day.
BILLY:	*(Shyly)* Jesus won't want me to talk to him. I'm a real silly Billy!
LEADER:	He does. He wants to talk to

	you, and he wants you to talk to him.
BERTIE:	So we can have a proper chat. How fascinating!
LEADER:	Some people are going to help us all pray now. Why don't you say 'Amen' at the end of the prayer to show you agree with what's being said?

PART THREE

BERTIE:	Well, that really is terribly exciting! Do you know what we've learnt today, Billy?
BILLY:	*(Goes to answer confidently, then…)* No.
BERTIE:	We've learnt that we can know Jesus without actually meeting him in person.
BILLY:	That's right!
BERTIE:	We don't really need a time machine to learn about God's heroes. Because they're all in here. *(Holds up Bible)*
BILLY:	Yes! And we can talk to God and God can talk to us today.
BERTIE:	And we're in a church full of God's heroes. That's terribly exciting!

Reproduced with permission from *Launchpad* published by BRF 2004 (1 84101 326 9)

LEADER:	*(Enters with some stickers)* Do you know what that means, Billy and Bertie? Because you follow Jesus and do what he wants, you're God's heroes as well!
BILLY:	Us! No, that's not right!
BERTIE:	I say, I think you've made a ghastly mistake! God's heroes were people like Joshua and Samuel, Esther and Jonah.
BILLY:	Yeah! And vicars and people who come to church like you lot! *(To congregation)*
LEADER:	No, you're God's heroes as well, if you do what God wants.
BERTIE:	That's a terribly interesting concept! *(To congregation)* Do you think we're God's heroes as well? *(Congregation responds)*
LEADER:	I've got some stickers for you here, which say that you are God's heroes! *(Sticks them on Billy and Bertie)*
BILLY:	That's fantastic! I'm going to wear it all week at school!
BERTIE:	There seem to be plenty more to go around! *(To congregation)* Tell you what, we'll give you all a sticker as you go out. What do you think, Billy?
BILLY:	Yeah! I'd like that!
BERTIE:	Come on then, Billy!

Billy and Bertie go to church door and give out stickers to the congregation as they leave.

Reproduced with permission from *Launchpad* published by BRF 2004 (1 84101 326 9)

LIVING IN HARMONY

Children love puppets. This series uses them to explore Christian living. Each puppet has a different character. Within each service, they learn something new about living in harmony.

Large puppets bought from specialist suppliers can be expensive. It is just as easy to use teddy bears or glove puppets. Rather than buying a full-size puppet theatre, you could throw a sheet over a clothes horse. The puppeteers will also be speaking the lines, so put a microphone in your puppet theatre.

You can hide your script in the puppet theatre, but rehearsal is still important.

The issues studied and relevant Bible passages are:

1. Saying sorry (Matthew 18:21–35): We need to learn to say sorry and forgive each other.

2. It's the inside that matters (Galatians 3:26–29; 1 Samuel 16:1–13): God doesn't judge people by the way they look on the outside, and neither should we.

3. The body of Christ (1 Corinthians 12:12–30): We are all good at different things and we are all important.

Saying sorry

 Teaching point

We need to learn to say sorry and forgive each other.

 Bible passage

Matthew 18:21–35.

 Key verse

Be kind and merciful, and forgive others, just as God forgave you because of Christ.

EPHESIANS 4:32

 Visual aids

Props to signify fifty million silver coins and one hundred silver coins

SERVICE FRAMEWORK

★ ★
★   ★
★   **Welcome the congregation.**   ★
★   ★
★ ★

Song

Sing the *Launchpad* song. (The congregation may have to learn it first.)

Talk outline

 Ask the children about their friends and what kind of things they like doing together. Are they always friends with each other or do they sometimes argue? It's difficult to be good friends all the time, because we sometimes annoy each other. We're going to talk about that today. First we're going to sing about our friends.

Song

Shake a friend's hand (KS: 293)

Puppets

The Mars bar problem *(see pages 50–52 for script)*.

Talk outline

 What happened every time someone got a Mars bar? Has anything like that ever happened at school? When someone picks on you, we call it bullying. People who are bigger than you sometimes think they can order you around, steal your things or call you names. They might even pick fights with you.

Lots of us get bullied at school. Don't worry if it happens to you. If you've been bullied, or seen other people bullied, who do you think you should tell? Sometimes we're scared about telling, because we think the bully will be angry with us and hurt us. But it's important to tell somebody, otherwise it can get worse. Remember Millicent, Lambert and Rupert. They told *(insert narrator's name)* about it, didn't they? And *(narrator)* told Crocodile not to do it any more.

Sometimes, it's not us who are being bullied. Maybe we're the bully. We pick on someone smaller or younger at school, or our little brother or sister at home. Sometimes we're rough and make them cry. What should we do when that happens? Just like the crocodile, we have to say sorry.

Confession

Lord Jesus, forgive us for those times when we let you down by bullying other people who are younger or smaller than we are. Help us to learn to live together in the way that you would like. Amen.

Lord Jesus, help us when we are being bullied by other people who are older or bigger. Help us to know the right thing to do. Help us to learn to live together in the way that you would like. Amen.

Song

I'm accepted, I'm forgiven (KS: 140) or
I'm sorry for the wrong I've done (KS: 161)

Activity

 Dramatize Matthew 18:21–35, asking the children to take the various parts and using props signifying the different amounts of money. Alternatively, use the script of 'The Unforgiving Servant' from *Time to Act*, or read the story from a children's Bible.

Talk outline

 The king is like God, and the money is like the wrong things we do. There are lots of things we've done wrong, but God forgives us. When someone has done something a little bit wrong to us, it's like they owe us a small amount of money. We can sometimes be like the servant and refuse to forgive others. That's not right. Because of the huge amount God has forgiven us, we should be ready to forgive others.

Final song

Lord, I lift your name on high (KS: 234)

Launchpad song plays as the congregation leaves.

The Mars bar problem

 Cast

Narrator (*stands in front of puppet theatre, talks to puppets and children*)
Millicent (*quite girly*)
Rupert (*quite snobbish*)
Lambert (*a wimp*)
Crocodile (*a bully*)

Other names can be used, depending on types of puppets available.

 Props

Four Mars bars

Script devised by The Oxford Area Schools Team (TOAST) and used with permission.

NARRATOR:	I've got some special friends I'd like you to meet. And I've got some presents for them. (*Holds up four Mars bars. To children*) Would you like to meet my friends? First, let's meet Millicent. Are you there, Millicent?

Children shout Millicent's name until she appears.

MILLICENT:	Hello, everyone!
NARRATOR:	I've got a present for you. Do you like Mars bars?
MILLICENT:	Mmm! I love Mars bars! They're lovely.
NARRATOR:	Here you are. (*Gives Mars bar*) Don't eat it all at once.
MILLICENT:	Mmm. I must watch out for Crocodile. He loves Mars bars, and eats them in one bite.
NARRATOR:	We'll have to warn Millicent if Crocodile is coming, won't we? (*Children respond. Enter Crocodile while Narrator is facing children*) If you can see Crocodile, make sure you shout out. (*Crocodile advances slowly. Children shout. Narrator pretends not to hear them*) What's that? Is Crocodile there?

Crocodile pounces on Millicent, snatches Mars bar and exits before Narrator turns around.

MILLICENT:	Oh no! He got my Mars bar. (*Bursts into tears and exits*)
NARRATOR:	Oh dear. Millicent was upset. Never mind. I've got three more Mars bars. Here's one for Lambert. Are you there, Lambert?

Enter Lambert.

LAMBERT: Hello! Ooh, is that a Mars bar? I like Mars bars!

NARRATOR: Yes, and this one's for you. *(Gives it to him)*

LAMBERT: Thank you very much! I'm going to save it for later.

NARRATOR: Watch out, Lambert. Crocodile likes Mars bars. He stole Millicent's. Make sure he doesn't get yours.

LAMBERT: Oh dear! I don't like the sound of that!

Enter Crocodile as Narrator turns to speak to the children.

NARRATOR: Warn Lambert if Crocodile is coming. *(Crocodile sneaks up on Lambert. Children shout out)* What's that? Can you see Crocodile? *(Narrator turns around. Crocodile disappears)* What are you talking about? He's not there! *(Narrator turns back towards children. Crocodile reappears at other*

end of puppet theatre) But do warn us if you see Crocodile, won't you?

Crocodile snatches Mars bar from Lambert.

LAMBERT: Aaarrgghh!! Crocodile got my Mars bar! It's not fair! *(Bursts into tears and exits)*

NARRATOR: Oh dear. That wasn't very nice, was it? Well, I've got another Mars bar here for Rupert. Are you there, Rupert?

Enter Rupert, haughtily.

RUPERT: Yes? What is it?

NARRATOR: Rupert, I've got a special present, just for you.

RUPERT: Don't patronize me, young man! What is it?

NARRATOR: It's a Mars bar! Do you like them?

RUPERT: They're OK, I suppose—but bad for your teeth.

NARRATOR: Would you like it?

RUPERT: I could take it off your hands, if you insist.

NARRATOR: I must just warn you, Rupert…

RUPERT: I know! Crocodile has been stealing Mars bars. I've just seen Millicent and Lambert.

NARRATOR: Well, I'm just warning you to watch out.

RUPERT: Don't worry. He won't get mine!

Enter Crocodile.

NARRATOR: *(Turns to children)* Now, you will warn us if you see Crocodile, won't you? *(Children shout)* Where? Where's Crocodile? *(He turns around. Crocodile disappears)* I can't see him. Can you, Rupert?

RUPERT: Absolutely not. I'm going to enjoy my Mars bar in peace, thank you.

NARRATOR: The coast is clear. No crocodiles anywhere. *(Narrator turns back to children. Enter Crocodile on other side. Children shout)* Where is it? *(Crocodile hides behind Rupert)* No—that's just Rupert!

Crocodile leaps on Rupert, steals Mars bar and exits.

RUPERT: I say! That bally Crocodile has gone and stolen my Mars bar!
NARRATOR: Oh dear. Well, I'm sorry, Rupert. I have one more Mars bar, but I can't give it to you, I'm afraid.
RUPERT: Hmph. You can keep it! *(Exits)*
NARRATOR: I've got one more Mars bar. It's for Crocodile. Shall we call him? *(Children call him)* Hello, Crocodile!

Crocodile appears, looking the worse for wear.

CROCODILE: Ughh!
NARRATOR: Hello, Crocodile! What's wrong with you? You don't look well.
CROCODILE: I don't feel well.
NARRATOR: Oh dear. What's the matter?
CROCODILE: I think I'm going to be sick!
NARRATOR: And why's that?
CROCODILE: I've eaten too many Mars bars.
NARRATOR: Oh dear. Well, I have a present for you. It's another Mars bar.
CROCODILE: Ughh! Not another one! Now I feel even worse.
NARRATOR: You weren't very nice, were you, Crocodile? You stole Mars bars from Lambert, Millicent and Rupert. What should you do about it?
CROCODILE: Don't know.
NARRATOR: *(To children)* What do you think he should do? *(They say, 'Say sorry')* Shall we call the rest of them back? Lambert! Millicent! Rupert! *(They all appear)*
RUPERT: What is all this fuss?

MILLICENT: Oh, it's that horrid Crocodile again!
LAMBERT: I'm a bit scared of him!
NARRATOR: Crocodile has something to say to you all. Go on, Crocodile!
CROCODILE: Hmph. Well, I'm sorry for stealing your Mars bars. I ate so many, it made me sick. You can all share mine if you like!
MILLICENT: Can we, Crocodile? That would be lovely!
RUPERT: OK, we forgive you. Don't do it again!
LAMBERT: You shouldn't bully us. Just because you've got sharp teeth!
CROCODILE: I've learnt my lesson. I'm going to give you all a piece of my Mars bar. Goodbye, everyone!

They all disappear.

Reproduced with permission from *Launchpad* published by BRF 2004 (1 84101 326 9)

It's the inside that matters

 Teaching point

God doesn't judge people by the way they look on the outside, and neither should we. It's what's on the inside that counts.

 Bible passages

Galatians 3:26–29; 1 Samuel 16:1–13.

 Key verse

The Lord told Samuel: 'People judge others by what they look like, but I judge people by what is in their hearts.'

1 SAMUEL 16:7

 Visual aids

Tin of 'dog food' prepared as per instructions in Activity One below. You will need:

One Mars bar
Chocolate Angel Delight
Sticky tape
Tin-opener and spoon

Items of clothing or equipment to denote a trade such as a church minister, doctor, soldier or cleaner (see Activity Two below)

off a tin of dog food and wrap it around the first tin.

Enter the church holding the tin so that the children can't see the tape. Ask if anyone is hungry. Hold up the tin and say it is your favourite food—solid, meaty nourishment. Open it with a tin-opener and start eating the contents with a spoon.

After a few spoonfuls, exit, promising to finish it later.

As an alternative activity, see 'Bubbles' on pages 32–33 of *Worship!*

SERVICE FRAMEWORK

★★★★★★★★★★★★★★★★★★★★★★★★★★★★★
★   ★
★   **Welcome the congregation.**   ★
★   ★
★★★★★★★★★★★★★★★★★★★★★★★★★★★★★

Song

Sing the *Launchpad* song.

Activity One

 Beforehand, carefully open the bottom of a tin of fruit, scrape out the contents and wash thoroughly. Fill with sliced Mars bars and chocolate Angel Delight. Tape up the tin. Peel the label

Puppets

Down with the greens! *(see pages 55–57 for script)*

Talk outline

 Recap the drama, emphasizing that Millicent, Rupert and Lambert didn't like Crocodile because of the colour of his skin. That was silly. But people sometimes do that—they decide what they think about someone because of what they look like, or because of their skin colour. Silly, isn't it? It's what's inside that matters. Which is more important to God—what you look like or what's inside?

Song

Everyone matters to Jesus (*The Big Book of Spring Harvest Kids' Praise*: 15)

Activity Two

 Invite some children to choose an item of clothing or a piece of equipment to denote people they might consider important— a high-ranking soldier, a doctor, a church minister and

so on—but one should be a manual worker like a dustman, painter or cleaner. Ask who is most important to God. Emphasize that God doesn't treat people differently because of what they wear or what job they do—and neither should we.

Song

Some people are fat (KS: 302)

Reading

Read 1 Samuel 16:1–13 (or tell the story from a children's Bible).

Talk outline

 Recap the story of how David was chosen to be king, emphasizing that God didn't look at outside appearances, but what was in David's heart.

Song

Look into my heart, Lord *(see Appendix pages 124–130 for words and music score)*

Prayers

Ask God to help us to stop judging people by what they look like or what job they do. Pray for any local initiatives against racism or to combat prejudice.

Activity One (continued)

 The team member who pretended to eat dog food returns to reveal what it really was. Emphazise that everyone thought it was dog food because that's what it said on the tin, but it was what was on the inside that mattered.

Final song

Make me a channel of your peace (KS: 248)

Launchpad song plays as the congregation leaves.

Down with the greens!

Script by Diana Nairne. Used with permission.

NARRATOR: *(To children)* What's your favourite colour? *(Children respond)* Why's that? *(Children respond)* I wonder if Millicent, Rupert and Lambert have favourite colours. Shall we ask them? Lambert! *(Enter Lambert)* Hello! You're looking smart today.

LAMBERT: I've got my brand new top on, and I really like it.

NARRATOR: We were just talking about our favourite colours. What's yours?

LAMBERT: I like blue. Blue is the colour of my new top. And blue is the colour of the sky on a lovely sunny day.

NARRATOR: That's true, Lambert. I wonder what colour Millicent likes best. *(Enter Millicent)* Hello. How are you today?

MILLICENT: I'm happy today, because it's my birthday.

NARRATOR: Is it? Happy birthday, Millicent!

MILLICENT: Yes, and I got really nice presents. I got a pony with a blue mane, and a make-up set with blue eyeshadow, and a tea set.

NARRATOR: Right. And what colour is the tea set?

MILLICENT: It's blue!

NARRATOR: We were just talking about favourite colours. I think yours must be…

MILLICENT: Blue! That's my favourite! Look at my dungarees—they're blue too! Oh, and *(insert narrator's name, if male)*…

 Cast

Narrator
Millicent
Rupert
Lambert
Crocodile

Clearly this sketch works best if one of the puppets is a different colour from all the rest—and it doesn't have to be green. But the same point can be made if three of the puppets are wearing similar coloured clothing. Adjust the script as necessary.

Props

Blue/green clothes
Blue football top or scarf for local team

Reproduced with permission from *Launchpad* published by BRF 2004 (1 84101 326 9)

NARRATOR:	Yes, Millicent?
MILLICENT:	I like blue because it's the colour of your eyes!
NARRATOR:	*(Embarrassed)* Er… yes, so we've established that your favourite colour is blue, Millicent. Thank you. What do you think Rupert's favourite colour is? *(Enter Rupert wearing football top or football scarf of team that plays in blue)* Hello! Are you just off to watch the football?
RUPERT:	Absolutely!
NARRATOR:	So if you support *(insert name of team)*, that means that your favourite colour is…
RUPERT:	Blue, naturally!
NARRATOR:	So… everyone's favourite colour is blue.
LAMBERT:	Yes, and look—Rupert's wearing blue trousers as well. So we're all wearing blue.
MILLICENT:	Ooh! We could form a blue gang, and wear blue all the time.
RUPERT:	Absolutely!
LAMBERT:	Do you know what colour I hate? I don't like green.
MILLICENT:	Ughh, no. Green. That's horrible!
NARRATOR:	Oh dear. Why don't you like green?
RUPERT:	It's horrible! It's the colour of salad. And green vegetables.
LAMBERT:	It's the colour of apples and pears and watermelons. I don't like any of them. I'd rather have a raspberry-flavoured slush puppy. Mm! That's nice and blue.
MILLICENT:	Yes, and green is the colour of snot! *(They all laugh)* Our blue gang won't be friends with anyone who wears green! Wouldn't that be cool? *(Chants)* Down with the greens! Down with the greens! *(Others join in)* Down with the greens!

Enter Crocodile.

CROCODILE:	Hello, everyone!
ALL:	Ughh! Green! Down with the greens! Down with the greens!
MILLICENT:	You're a horrible green crocodile, and we're not going to talk to you!
LAMBERT:	Yeah! Go away, you greenie!
RUPERT:	Go and eat lettuce and celery and leeks and broccoli with your other green friends! We're having a blue gang meeting!

Millicent, Rupert and Lambert exit.

NARRATOR:	Oh dear. I'm sorry, Crocodile. We were just talking about our favourite colours, and it got out of hand.
CROCODILE:	They've stopped being my friends! Just because I'm green! I'm going to cry…

Crocodile exits, crying.

NARRATOR:	*(To children)* Oh dear. That wasn't nice, was it? They decided that they didn't like Crocodile because he was green. They didn't want to be

Reproduced with permission from *Launchpad* published by BRF 2004 (1 84101 326 9)

with him because of the colour of his skin! Now, that sounds really silly, doesn't it? But sometimes we're a bit like that. None of us has green skin, but people do have black, brown or white skin. All people are all different in one way or another, and sometimes we're nasty to others because they don't look like us, like Millicent, Rupert and Lambert were to Crocodile. Sometimes we have our own gangs and we don't let other people join in. But whoever you are, it's silly not to be friends with someone because they're different, isn't it? Do you think Millicent, Rupert and Lambert were being silly? I think we should call them back, don't you? Millicent, Lambert, Rupert! Where are you?

They all appear.

RUPERT:	You've just interrupted our blue club meeting.
NARRATOR:	Well, we were just talking out here, and we think your blue club is a silly idea.
MILLICENT:	No, it's not! We'll have exciting blue things to do. Like looking at blue sky, and painting our bedrooms blue…
LAMBERT:	…and lying on the blue grass and looking at the blue leaves on the trees…
NARRATOR:	Wait a minute, Lambert! The grass isn't blue! *(To children)* What colour is the grass? *(Children say 'Green!')* And what colour are the leaves on the trees? *(Children say 'Green!')*
LAMBERT:	Oh yes! So they are!
NARRATOR:	You do like things that are green, after all!

LAMBERT:	I suppose we do.
NARRATOR:	And aren't there other things that you like that are green? What about mint-flavoured ice-cream?
MILLICENT:	Oh, yes! I like that!
NARRATOR:	And wobbly green jelly! And big, green dinosaurs! And gooseberries! And grapes!
RUPERT:	Absolutely! We like all of those.
LAMBERT:	Yes, we do!
NARRATOR:	And what about the green Crocodile? You like him really, too, don't you?
ALL:	Yes, we do! We like Crocodile really!
NARRATOR:	You need to say sorry to him, don't you? *(They nod)* Shall we call him back? Crocodile, where are you? *(Encourage children to shout for him. Enter Crocodile, reluctantly)* The others want to say something to you, Crocodile.
MILLICENT:	Sorry for picking on you, Crocodile. Just because you're green.
LAMBERT:	We like green things, really.
RUPERT:	Yes. And we're not going to have a blue club any more.
CROCODILE:	Oh, thank you.
MILLICENT:	Would you like to come and play with us?
CROCODILE:	Yes, I would!
ALL:	Come on, then! Bye, everyone!

All exit.

Reproduced with permission from *Launchpad* published by BRF 2004 (1 84101 326 9)

The body of Christ

 Teaching point
We are all good at different things and we are all important.

 Bible passage
1 Corinthians 12:12–30.

 Key verse
Together you are the body of Christ. Each one of you is part of his body.
1 CORINTHIANS 12:27

 Visual aids
Clear OHP acetates
Roll of plain lining paper
Pencils or crayons
Camcorder and data projector/TV *(optional)*
Sheets of A4 copy paper
Percussion instruments
Card
Glue stick
Finger-paints
Kitchen towel or hand wipes

SERVICE FRAMEWORK

★★★★★★★★★★★★★★★★★★★★★★★★★★★★
★ **Welcome the congregation.** ★
★★★★★★★★★★★★★★★★★★★★★★★★★★★★

Song

Sing the *Launchpad* song.

Talk outline

 Ask children what they're good at. Write answers on OHP acetate. Today, we're thinking about everyone being good at something, whoever they are… *(interrupted by puppets)*

Puppets

Everyone matters *(see page 60–62 for script)*.

Talk outline

 Sometimes we feel like Millicent. We think we're no good at anything, but everyone else seems to be really good at things. The good news is that we all matter to God, whether we're good at football or can't play for toffee; whether we do our homework fast like Rupert, or can't do it at all, like Millicent. And, if you look really carefully, you'll find something you can do really well.

Song

Everyone matters to Jesus (*The Big Book of Spring Harvest Kids' Praise*: 15)

Talk outline

 The Bible says that the church is like the body of Christ. That means we all have different things to do, just like different parts of the body. There's no point my eye saying, 'I want to walk!' because

it can't on its own. Demonstrate. There's no point my leg saying, 'I want to see!', because it can't on its own. Demonstrate. All the different parts of the body work together so that you can walk and see at the same time.

Activity

We want to show you how good you all are at doing all sorts of things and working together. We're going to divide up into groups to do different things, then get back together and show each other what we've done. Choose which group to go into.

Suggested tasks for each group *(each is designed for children and adults to do together)*:

- Art: Paint a picture, or create a collage of a life-size body. Draw around a person lying on a sheet of paper. Everybody else decorates parts of the body.

- Video: Make a video using a camcorder. You could dramatize what has to be done to make sure services happen each week, with people playing themselves or others. Alternatively, everyone thinks about the talents there are in the church and each says one in turn to camera.

- Prayer: Prepare prayers for later in the service, thanking God for the talents in the church and asking him to help people to work together better in the future.

- Music: Learn a new song to teach to the congregation, learn special harmonies to a familiar song, or learn some percussion or instrumental accompaniment to a familiar song.

- Craft: Make a cardboard cut-out of the church building and fill it with fingerprints, using paint or a fingerprinting set, to represent the body of Christ.

You may have other ideas! A team member takes charge of each group to help its members keep to the task in hand. Encourage as many people as possible to participate in the groups, but allow people to opt out if they want. Allow 20 minutes or so before bringing everyone together. The rest of the service depends on each group's contributions.

- Song: Music group teaches the congregation the song they have learnt.

- Art and craft: The art and craft is displayed and explained.
- Video: The video is played on the data projector or on TV screens.
- Prayers: The group that prepared prayers leads the intercessions.

Alternative activities

'On Yer Bike' from page 223 of *100 Worship Activities for Children* or read 'The Dream Team' from page 36 of *50 Stories for Special Occasions*.

Talk outline

Everyone matters in our church. Everyone has a part to play. You've all played a part in today's *Launchpad*. Well done!

Final song

For I'm building a people of power (KS: 61)

Launchpad song plays as congregation leaves.

Everyone matters

 Cast

Narrator
Millicent
Rupert
Lambert
Crocodile

 Props

Two recorders *(one for Lambert and one to play backstage)*

Card showing words of 'God's love is like a circle'

Script devised by The Oxford Area Schools Team (TOAST) and used with permission.

NARRATOR:	Everyone is good at something, whoever they are. Some of you here may be good at reading, or swimming, or jumping…
MILLICENT:	*(Interrupts by shouting name of narrator)*
NARRATOR:	Excuse me a minute. What is it, Millicent?
MILLICENT:	*(Pathetically)* You said everyone is good at something. I'm no good at anything!
NARRATOR:	I'm sure you are!
MILLICENT:	No. I can't do anything at all. I'm no good to anyone.
NARRATOR:	Well, let's think carefully and see if we can find something you are good at, shall we?

Enter Crocodile, running continuously along the length of the puppet theatre.

MILLICENT:	Ooh, what are you doing, Crocodile?
CROCODILE:	I'm training for a marathon. I've got to run seventeen miles every day.
MILLICENT:	A marathon! Can I join in, please, Crocodile? Maybe I could run in a marathon.
CROCODILE:	You'll have to keep up with me.

Millicent runs behind Crocodile, but is slower and keeps being lapped.

MILLICENT:	*(Puffing and panting)* I'm not as fast as you, Crocodile! I'm no good at this.
CROCODILE:	You couldn't run a marathon, Millicent. Right, I've got to run twenty-five times up and down

Reproduced with permission from *Launchpad* published by BRF 2004 (1 84101 326 9)

(insert name of local street).
See you later!

Crocodile exits.

MILLICENT: See! I'm no good at running. I
told you!
NARRATOR: Perhaps there's something else
you could do.

Enter Rupert, haughtily.

RUPERT: Hello, Millicent.
MILLICENT: Hello, Rupert.
RUPERT: Do you want to come out? I've
finished my homework already.
MILLICENT: You've finished? I haven't
started! I can't do it!
RUPERT: I got ten out of ten in spelling
today and ten out of ten in
sums. It's dead easy.
MILLICENT: I only got two out of ten in
spelling! I'm no good at maths
either. There's nothing I'm
good at.
RUPERT: Well, I'm going to do some
extra homework now, so I'll get
the best marks again tomorrow.
Goodbye!

Rupert exits.

MILLICENT: See! I'm not brainy like Rupert.
I'm no good at anything.
NARRATOR: We'll find something, Millicent.
(Enter Lambert with recorder)
What's that?
MILLICENT: It's Lambert's recorder. He's
always playing it.
LAMBERT: Hello, Millicent! Do you want to
hear the tune I've learnt how to
play?
MILLICENT: Oh yes! What is it?

*Lambert pretends to play 'God's love is like a
circle'—to the tune of 'Puff the Magic Dragon'. It's
really played inside puppet theatre on second
recorder.*

MILLICENT: That was great, Lambert! I wish
I could play the recorder. Can I
have a go?
LAMBERT: Yes, OK.

*Narrator gives Millicent recorder. She tries to play,
but makes a terrible noise.*

MILLICENT: Oh, Lambert! I can't do that
either!
LAMBERT: Well, I'm going to carry on
practising. I'm going to be in
the school band!

Lambert exits.

MILLICENT: I can't play musical instruments.
I'll never get to be in the band.
And I'll never get top marks at
maths and spelling. And I'll
never run a marathon. I just
can't do anything!
NARRATOR: I'm still thinking, Millicent! I'm
sure there's something you can
do that Lambert, Rupert and
Crocodile can't. Tell you what—
while we're thinking, why don't

we teach everybody the song that Lambert was playing?

NARRATOR: Why don't we teach everyone? Oh, but we haven't got any words.

MILLICENT: Well, Crocodile is good at running, so he could run and get some card…

CROCODILE: And Rupert is good at spelling, so he could write it out…

RUPERT: And Lambert is good on the recorder, so he could play it…

LAMBERT: And Millicent is good at singing, so she could sing it…!

They run off, produce the card showing the words, and all sing song. Narrator encourages congregation to join in.

MILLICENT: 'God's love is like a circle'? You don't want to learn that, do you? Oh, all right, then.

*God's love is like a circle
A circle big and round
And when you have a circle
No ending can be found.
And so the love of Jesus
Goes on eternally,
And when I draw a circle
I know that he loves me.*

She sings beautifully. Lambert, Rupert and Crocodile appear as she finishes.

CROCODILE: Gosh, Millicent! We heard some really good singing!

MILLICENT: That was me!

NARRATOR: You see, Millicent, there is something you're good at! You're good at singing! Isn't she good, everyone?

MILLICENT: Ooh! I hadn't thought of that!

Reproduced with permission from *Launchpad* published by BRF 2004 (1 84101 326 9)

JESTER'S TALES

This three-part series looks at the life of David through the eyes of a jester from his court. It places fewer demands on a church to produce a group of competent actors, but requires two strong performers to hold it together. One plays Chester (or Esther) the Jester, who tells the stories. The other is the service leader.

The services also feature original songs about David (see Appendix, pages 120–157). As they often include two singing parts, both the main performers should be able to sing well. The teaching points are explored in dialogue between the two. You are free to expand on the outlines given.

The issues studied and relevant Bible passages are:

1. The good shepherd (1 Samuel 16:1–13; John 10:11–15): Samuel anoints shepherd-boy David to be the next king. Jesus protects us, just as David protected his sheep.

2. The faithful soldier (1 Samuel 17:1–51; Deuteronomy 1:31): David defeats Goliath by trusting in God. Through faith in God, we can face our problems.

3. The great king (1 Samuel 24:1–22; 2 Samuel 5:1–5; Jeremiah 29:11): David refuses to kill Saul and take the throne until the time is right; he eventually becomes a great king. God is also preparing us for the future.

The good shepherd

 Teaching point

Jesus protects us, just as David protected his sheep.

 Bible passages

1 Samuel 16:1–13; John 10:11–15.

 Key verse

I am the good shepherd. I know my sheep, and they know me.

JOHN 10:14

 Visual aids

Cue cards: David—hurrah!; farm—ooh, aah!; sheep—baa!; scary—aagh!

Cardboard sheep with fragments of the key verse on them, including reference *(see activity, p. 66)*. Trace or photocopy the templates on pages 67–69.

SERVICE FRAMEWORK

★★★★★★★★★★★★★★★★★★★★★★★★★★★★★
★   ★
★   **Welcome the congregation.**   ★
★   ★
★★★★★★★★★★★★★★★★★★★★★★★★★★★★★

Song

Sing the *Launchpad* song.

Talk outline

 Explain that a special guest is coming. He's a jester from the court of King David. Ask the congregation to join you in calling for him. Chester enters carrying a spotted hanky on a stick, containing juggling balls.

Introduce Chester and ask him to juggle. Chester is reluctant and asks for a child to do it instead. After the child's demonstration, Chester attempts it and drops the balls. A similar thing happens when he is asked to turn cartwheels.

Ask how he entertained King David. Chester explains that David listened to stories and songs. Ask Chester to tell a story.

Story

The congregation join in with responses to the words in **bold**. Practise them before telling the story. Cue words and responses: **David**—hurrah!; **farm**—ooh, aah!; **sheep**—baa!; **scary**—aagh!

 A long time ago, before **David** was made king, he worked on Jesse's **farm**. Jesse was his dad. All his brothers were older than him. 'Little squirt', they called **David**. His brothers got all the best jobs around the **farm**. So who do you think had the worst job of all? Yes, it was **David**. He had to look after his father's **sheep**.

The job was quite **scary**, being out on his own with them, but nobody took better care of those **sheep** than **David**. He knew every single one of them by name, even though there were a hundred of them. The **sheep** knew his voice, and when they heard him call, they knew they were safe because they were around **David**.

One day, on his dad's **farm**, there was a **scary** storm. It scattered all the **sheep**. They were all running around and bleating. **David** called out to them and managed to round them up again. He counted them.

'…97, 98, 99… I knew it!' said **David**. 'I'm missing one of my **sheep**!'

He ran inside and picked up his staff and his sling. Then he ran into the **scary** storm and out into the hills around the **farm**.

David soon picked up the **sheep's** tracks. Suddenly he heard a noise. He stopped and strained to hear. It was the bleating of a **sheep**.

But a lion had heard it too and was bounding down the hill. How **scary**! **David** charged at the lion, shook his staff and shouted really loudly. He hit the **scary** lion on the head with his staff. It fell to the ground and didn't move again. But the **scary** lion wasn't the only one to hear the **sheep**. A huge bear was now bounding up the track. **David** reached for his sling.

He plucked a stone from the ground and dropped it into the sling. Round and round his head the sling whirled, and then… zing! The stone went flying through the air and hit the **scary** bear. The bear turned around and ran away, growling as it went.

David cheered, then picked up the frightened **sheep**. He carried it all the way home to his dad's **farm**. That night, they invited all their neighbours round and had a big party to celebrate the safe return of the hundredth **sheep**.

Alternative story

Perform 'The Lost Sheep' from *Red Letter Days*.

Song

There were ninety-nine sheep (KS: 333)

Talk outline

 Chester explains that David was Jesse's youngest son and so had all the worst jobs. Chester thinks that sheep are dirty and smelly and wouldn't like to be a shepherd. Ask if the job was dangerous. Chester explains how David fought off lions and bears. Ask if David was a good shepherd. Chester says that David looked after his sheep, he knew them by name and they knew him too. Make the point that Jesus is also a good shepherd, that he came looking for us and rescued us, just as David rescued his hundredth sheep. Chester says that that must have been dangerous. Explain how it cost Jesus everything, but explain how he protects us, like David protected his sheep.

Song

I will search for my lost sheep *(see pages 120–123)*

This song is performed by Chester. The congregation joins in the chorus.

Talk outline

 Ask Chester how David became a king if he was just a shepherd. Chester explains that the previous king, called Saul, wasn't doing what God wanted. God decided to choose a new king and sent a messenger called Samuel to Jesse, David's dad. Ask Chester how excited David was about that. Chester says that David was still looking after his sheep when Samuel came. Jesse thought it would be one of his seven oldest sons who was chosen to be king.

Song

Look into my heart, Lord *(see pages 124–130)*

This song is performed by Chester and service leader.

Talk outline

 Samuel got it wrong too, didn't he? Chester agrees, explaining that when Samuel saw how strong David's brothers were, he was also sure that God would choose one of them. Ask Chester why God chose David. Chester explains that God knew David would care for his people just like he'd cared for his sheep. God judged by what was in David's heart instead of what he looked like.

Explain to Chester that the same applies to him—that it doesn't matter that he can't juggle or do cartwheels. Chester is excited by this. Tell him that David chose him to be the court jester because he was special. Chester doesn't understand. Tell Chester that he's special because he can sing and tell stories. Ask him to return with more next time. Chester agrees enthusiastically and exits.

Confession

Rehearse the congregation's response beforehand.

LEADER:	Dear God, we are sorry for the times when we wander away from you. When we stop reading the Bible, we can't hear your voice. When we stop praying, we stop talking to you. *(Pause)* Good shepherd…
ALL:	**Rescue, heal and protect us.**
LEADER:	Dear God, we are sorry for the times when we do things that we shouldn't. It can be hard to do what you ask sometimes and so we do wrong things instead, but the wrong things we do only end up hurting us. *(Pause)* Good shepherd…
ALL:	**Rescue, heal and protect us.**
LEADER:	Dear God, we are sorry for the times when we only want to make friends with people who look cool. We're sorry for the times when we haven't wanted to be friends with people who can't do things that everyone else can. *(Pause)* Good shepherd…
ALL:	**Rescue, heal and protect us.**
LEADER:	Loving God, rescue us when we wander off, heal us when we hurt ourselves and protect us from all those things that take us away from you; through Jesus, our good shepherd.
ALL:	**Amen.**

Song

God is good (KS: 74)

Activity

 Using the templates provided, make large cardboard sheep showing fragments of John 10:14, and scatter them around the church beforehand. Ask for volunteers—one child for each sheep. Explain that the sheep in the story were scattered and needed rescuing, just like us. Send the children to rescue the sheep. When they return, rearrange the fragments and read the verse with the congregation. Keep reading, taking a sheep away each time through until the congregation has memorized the verse.

Prayers

Pray that Jesus will find his lost sheep. Pray that world leaders will do what God wants, unlike Saul.

Final hymn

The Lord's my shepherd (SOF2: 1030) or
The king of love my shepherd is (SOF: 533)

Launchpad song plays as congregation leaves.

I am the good shepherd.

I know my sheep,

and they
know me.

JOHN 10:14

The faithful soldier

Teaching point

Through faith in God, we can face our problems.

Bible passages

1 Samuel 17:1–51; Deuteronomy 1:31.

Key verse

You know that the Lord has taken care of us… just as you might carry one of your children.

DEUTERONOMY 1:31

Visual aids

Cue cards: David—hurrah!; Philistine(s)—boo; Goliath—Come and have a go, if you think you're hard enough!; squirt—picture of someone blowing a raspberry.

Cardboard armour with fragments of key verse on them, including reference *(see activity, p. 72)*.

Trace or photocopy templates on pages 73–75.

SERVICE FRAMEWORK

★★★★★★★★★★★★★★★★★★★★★★★★★★★★★
★   ★
★   **Welcome the congregation.**   ★
★   ★
★★★★★★★★★★★★★★★★★★★★★★★★★★★★★

Song

Sing the *Launchpad* song.

Talk outline

Ask children what they remember about Chester, and recap stories from previous *Launchpad*. Ask them to call Chester in again. He looks scared. Ask him what the problem is. Chester explains that he's been asked to juggle torches while walking on a tightrope. Say that that doesn't sound too hard. Chester reveals that they are flaming torches… and that he will be blindfolded… and that he's scared of the dark.

Ask Chester if he remembers a story about when David did something scary.

Story

Cue words and responses: **David**—hurrah!; **Philistine(s)** —boo; **Goliath**—Come and have a go, if you think you're hard enough!; **squirt**—blow raspberries.

One day, **David** was working with his dad on the farm.

'Your brothers have all gone off to join the army and fight the **Philistines**,' said his dad. 'But they've forgotten their packed lunch. Go and take it to them, and while you're there, find out how they're getting on.'

'All right, lads?' **David** said, when he eventually caught up with them.

'Clear off, **squirt**,' said his brothers. 'Can't you see we're going to fight the **Philistines**?'

Suddenly, a voice thundered: 'Come and have a go, if you think you're hard enough!'

Everyone stopped. Up ahead was the biggest **Philistine** soldier anyone had ever seen. He was at least nine feet tall. The Israelite soldiers all turned around and ran away—all of them except **David**.

'That **Philistine** isn't so tough,' said **David**. 'I'll fight him.'

It just so happened that King Saul overheard **David**.

'How could you fight **Goliath**?' the king said to **David**. 'You're just a little **squirt**!'

'I've killed lions and bears, looking after my dad's sheep,' **David** replied. 'God looked after me then, and he'll look after me now.'

'All right,' said Saul. 'You're on. God help you!'

Saul took his armour, his helmet and his sword, and put them all on **David**. But they were too big for **David** and he couldn't walk. He took them off and walked towards the giant with just his staff and sling.

'Oi, **Goliath**!' shouted **David**. 'I'll fight you!'

'What? You? You're just a little **squirt**!' thundered **Goliath**.

'You might be big and mean and quite scary,' said **David**, 'but God's on my side and I'll have you!'

'You're dead meat!' shouted **Goliath** as he walked towards **David**.

Our hero ran towards **Goliath**. He took a stone from his bag, dropped it into the sling, whirled it around his head and slung it. Zing! The stone flew through the air. Whack! It hit the giant right between the eyes. Ker-thud! He fell to the ground. That was the end of **Goliath**.

When they saw that their champion was defeated, the **Philistines** all ran away. The Israelites had won, all thanks to a little **squirt** called **David**.

Alternative story

Perform 'David and Goliath' from *Lightning Sketches*.

Song

Goliath (*Songs of Fellowship for Kids*: 46)

Talk outline

Recap on the story with children. Ask Chester whether David was afraid of Goliath, and why not. Ask for a small child and a tall adult to stand at the front. Ask the child to imagine someone who was twice as tall as the adult. Would they be frightened? Chester has an idea and puts the child on his shoulders. Explain that the child is now taller than the adult.

Because David trusted in God, it was like he was being carried on God's shoulders—so Goliath didn't look big and scary. Explain that if we trust in God, our problems won't look so big and scary. Explain to Chester that the same applies to his fear of walking a tightrope juggling while blindfolded.

Ask the children what things worry them. Make the point that God asks us to make a leap of faith too.

Song

One giant leap *(see pages 131–134)*

The song is performed by Chester and the service leader. The congregation joins in the chorus.

Talk outline

Chester explains that facing Goliath was not the only problem David faced. King Saul was jealous of David because everyone thought that David was a better soldier than he was. He even tried to kill David with his spear. But David still trusted in God.

Explain that sometimes we argue with our friends. But if we trust in God, he will help us. Chester says that God helped David by giving him a special friend—Jonathan, King Saul's son. Explain that God also gives us friends—in church, and in school—who can help us when we are worried.

Song

Saul has killed his thousands *(see pages 135–138)*

The song is performed by Chester and the service leader.

Talk outline

Chester says that David faced one problem after another, but trusted God. Point out that Chester should do the same and ask God to help him with his fears. Ask him to promise to return and tell you how he got on, and what happened to David next. Chester promises to—if he makes it! He exits.

Confession

Rehearse the response beforehand.

LEADER: Loving Father, you always want to help us. We are sorry for the times when we don't trust you. When there's a big problem in our lives, we forget to talk to you about it or ask you to help us. *(Pause)* Almighty God…

ALL: **Help us to listen to your voice.**

LEADER: Tender Christ, who came into the world as a helpless baby, we are sorry for the times when we pick on other people. When we think we're stronger than someone else, we sometimes call them names or try to hurt them. *(Pause)* Almighty God…

ALL: **Help us to listen to your voice.**

LEADER: Gentle Spirit, who never leaves us and carries us on his shoulders, we are sorry that we don't always do what you ask us to do. Sometimes we think, say or do things that we know are wrong. *(Pause)* Almighty God…

ALL: **Help us to listen to your voice.**

LEADER: God who gives strength to all, when we don't trust you, when we're unkind and when we hurt you through our actions, help us to listen to your voice, through Jesus, our brave defender.

ALL: **Amen.**

Song

Be bold, be strong (KS: 17)

Activity

Using the templates provided, make large cardboard pieces of armour showing fragments of Deuteronomy 1:31. Explain that Saul thought David would need lots of armour to fight Goliath. Encourage the congregation to learn the verse by reading it through, taking a piece away each time until they have memorized it. When all the pieces of armour have been removed, explain that David didn't need the armour. All he needed was to trust in God.

Prayers

Pray that God will show those who have problems that they can trust him.

Final song

Faithful one (SOF: 89)

Launchpad song plays as congregation leaves.

You know
that the Lord

Reproduced with permission from *Launchpad* published by BRF 2004 (1 84101 326 9)

has taken
care of us…
just as you

might carry one of your children.

DEUTERONOMY 1:31

The great king

 Teaching point

God is preparing us for the future.

 Bible passages

1 Samuel 24:1–22; 2 Samuel 5:1–5; Jeremiah 29:11.

 Key verse

I alone know the plans I have for you, plans to bring you prosperity and not disaster, plans to bring about the future you hope for.

JEREMIAH 29:11 (GNB)

 Visual aids

Photo of Lester the Jester downloaded from www.launchpad-services.com
OHP
Cue cards: desert—phew!; David—hurrah!;
Saul—Your majesty!; crying—boo hoo!
Cardboard crowns with fragments of key verse on them, including reference *(see activity, p.78)*. Trace or photocopy the templates on pages 79–81.

SERVICE FRAMEWORK

★★★★★★★★★★★★★★★★★★★★★★★★★★★★★
★   ★
★   **Welcome the congregation.**   ★
★   ★
★★★★★★★★★★★★★★★★★★★★★★★★★★★★★

Song

Sing the *Launchpad* song.

Talk outline

 Ask children what they remember about Chester and the stories he told about David. Remind them about his big challenge. Ask congregation to call Chester in, as before. He enters from the back of church to the *Rocky* theme ('Gonna Fly Now'

by Bill Conti), shaking hands as he walks triumphantly to the front.

Chester claims to have walked blindfolded on a tightrope, juggling flaming torches. Congratulate him and ask to see a photo. Chester flashes one in front of the children quickly. Ask for a proper look and discover that it's not him. Display photo (downloaded from www.launchpad-services.com) on OHP screen.

Chester admits he didn't do the challenge. Ask him if he asked God to help him. Chester says he didn't need to because his friend, Lester the Jester, offered to do it for him. Point out that Chester took the easy way out. Ask him if this is what David would have done. Chester concedes that David didn't, and tells the story.

Story

Cue words: **desert**—phew!; **David**—hurrah!; **Saul**—Your majesty!; **crying**—boo hoo!

 After **David** had killed Goliath, everyone in Israel said he would make a brilliant king. They loved him more than King **Saul**. **Saul** knew that the prophet Samuel had said that God had chosen **David** to be the next king. That was bad news for **Saul**.

He went around his palace **crying**. **Saul** threw his spear at **David**. Fortunately, he missed.

Our hero ran away. **Saul** heard that **David** was hiding in the **desert**, so he went there with three thousand men. They searched all day without finding him. It was a hot day in the **desert**, and they were going to go home.

King **Saul** said, 'I'm just going to the toilet.' In the **desert** there were no toilets, so **Saul** went into the nearest cave. But can you guess who was hiding at the back of that cave? It was

David. He was there hiding from the king with all his friends. When they saw **Saul** come in and hitch up his robe, they couldn't believe it!

'Now's your chance!' **David**'s friends said. 'Do him in!'

So **David** crept up behind **Saul**. He took out his sword and… cut off a piece of his robe! When **Saul** had finished going to the toilet, he adjusted his robe and noticed that it now had a big hole in it.

'Oh dear,' said **Saul**. 'My best robe.'

'Your majesty!' shouted **David**. He waved the patch of cloth. 'I had you in my power and didn't hurt you!'

Saul was amazed. Even though he'd tried to spear the young man, **David** had spared his life. Saul started **crying**.

'I'm really sorry I threw my spear at you,' sobbed **Saul**. 'You're much nicer than me. Perhaps you should be king after all.'

Then **David** started **crying**. Soon everyone was **crying**. So **Saul** let **David** and his followers go. And **Saul** was very careful after that, each time he went to the toilet.

Song

O Lord, you're great (KS: 270)

Talk outline

 Recap the story. Explain how God had promised David that he would be king. If he had killed Saul when he had the chance, he could have been king straight away. But Chester explains that David didn't want to harm Saul because he knew it wasn't right. David knew that God had a plan, so he didn't take the short cut.

Tell Chester that he did take a short cut by letting his friend do something he should have done. Chester admits he did, and that he should have trusted in God. Explain that it is difficult sometimes to trust that God has a plan for us when we have problems.

Ask what happened to Saul. Chester says that he went to war with the Philistines and was killed in battle. Ask if that made David happy because he could now be king. Chester says that it didn't, because he didn't want anything bad to happen to Saul. He was also sad because his friend Jonathan died in the same battle.

Song

David's lament *(see pages 139–142)*

The song is performed by Chester.

Talk outline

 Chester explains how sad David was that his friend Jonathan and King Saul wouldn't be around any more. He had always tried to help Saul, even though God had promised that David would be king. Ask what happened to David.

Reading

Read 2 Samuel 5:1–5.

Talk outline

 Share your excitement that David became king in the end—despite not taking a short cut. Chester says that David had to wait a long time, but always tried to do the right thing because he knew God had a plan for his life. Everything he went through helped to prepare David to be a great king.

Explain that God has a plan for all of us too, and that everything we go through helps us to become the kind of person God wants. Sometimes we argue with our friends, but when we make up, we learn how to be better friends in the future. Chester asks whether bad things

will still happen, even if we trust in God's plan. Explain that they will—as they happened to David—but that God helps us to learn through them. Ask Chester to remind us of what happened in David's life.

Song

Chester's medley *(see pages 143–157)*

The song is performed by Chester and the service leader.

Talk outline

Thank Chester for his stories and songs, wish him all the best as he discovers God's plan for his life, and encourage the children to say goodbye.

Confession

Rehearse the response beforehand.

Leader:	Eternal God, thank you that you have a plan for all our lives. Sometimes it's hard to do the right thing. We are sorry for the times when we try to take a short cut to get to where we want to go. *(Pause)* When we go the wrong way, God of promise…
All:	**Forgive us and lead us.**
Leader:	Jesus Christ, who forgave those who wounded you, thank you that you give us the strength to love others. We are sorry for the times when we want to hurt those who have hurt us. *(Pause)* When we do things that injure you, God of promise…
All:	**Forgive us and lead us.**
Leader:	Holy Spirit who teaches and trains us, thank you that you are preparing us for our future. We are sorry that we don't always see what you are doing. We are sometimes angry with you for the bad things that happen. *(Pause)* When we complain, God of promise…
All:	**Forgive us and lead us.**
Leader:	God who leads us through all our lives, when we take a short

cut, when we're unforgiving and when we grumble, show us the plan you have for us and help us to follow you through Jesus Christ, our Lord.

All: **Amen.**

Song

Blessed be the name of the Lord (SOF2: 673)

Activity

Using the templates provided, make large cardboard crowns showing fragments of Jeremiah 29:11. Encourage the congregation to learn the verse, as before.

Prayers

Pray that God will show people that he has a plan for their lives.

Final hymn

Be thou my vision (SOF: 42)

Launchpad song plays as the congregation leaves.

I alone know
the plans I have
for you,

plans to bring you
prosperity and
not disaster,

plans to bring
about the future
you hope for.

JEREMIAH 29:11 (GNB)

MEETING JESUS

This series focuses on who Jesus is and what happened on Good Friday and Easter Sunday. It could therefore be used leading up to Easter or in an Easter holiday club. In this series, we meet Jesus through three of his closest friends.

Each service involves a simple piece of drama. Two narrators read the script, while a small group mimes the actions suggested. The narration and miming should be within the capabilities of a youth group of 11- to 14-year-olds. The rhymes give each sketch a rhythm. There are also additional optional pieces of drama that can be used with this series, available on www.launchpad-services.com.

The themes, Bible passages and teaching points are:

1. Jesus' ministry: Matthew the tax collector, an unpopular man, is chosen by Jesus to be his friend. Encountering Jesus changes your life (Matthew 9:9–13). How do we do what Jesus wants?

2. Jesus' crucifixion: Peter lets Jesus down, but Jesus forgives him. He forgives us too when we do things that we know are wrong (Luke 22:54–62; John 21: 15–19).

3. Jesus' resurrection: Mary is the first to see Jesus alive again and rushes to tell her friends. Jesus offers new life to all (John 20:11–18). Are we excited enough by Jesus' resurrection to want to tell others (Matthew 28:16 20)?

Matthew: Jesus' ministry

 Teaching point

How do we do what Jesus wants?

 Bible passage

Matthew 9:9–13.

 Key verse

Jesus said, 'I didn't come to invite good people to be my followers. I came to invite sinners.'

MATTHEW 9:13

 Visual aids

None needed

SERVICE FRAMEWORK

★★★★★★★★★★★★★★★★★★★★★★★★★★★★★
★　　　　　　　　　　　　　　　　　　　　★
★　　　　**Welcome the congregation.**　　　★
★　　　　　　　　　　　　　　　　　　　　★
★★★★★★★★★★★★★★★★★★★★★★★★★★★★★

Song

Sing the *Launchpad* song. (The congregation may have to learn it first.)

Talk outline

 In this series, we'll meet some people who knew Jesus—people who were his best friends. How many of you have got best friends? Did you start out not liking them, and then become good friends? That's what happened with a man called Matthew.

Optional sketch: I want to be a millionaire

See www.launchpad-services.com for script.

Song

Jesus is greater than the greatest heroes (KS: 196)

Drama

Matthew meets Jesus *(see pages 86–87 for script)*.

Talk outline

 Recap the story, pointing out that even though people didn't like Matthew, Jesus wanted to be his friend. People weren't happy about it. They thought Jesus shouldn't eat with a person who cheated others. But Jesus knew that Matthew had changed. Matthew wanted to do what Jesus said.

Song

I am a new creation (KS: 115) or
I wanna be with you, Jesus (*The Big Book of Spring Harvest Kids' Praise*: 47)

Talk outline

 The exciting news is that Jesus wants to be our friend too. Sometimes we're like Matthew. We might not con people, but we do other things that Jesus doesn't like. We fight with our brothers and

sisters, we don't do what our mum and dad want, we greedily pinch the last piece of chocolate, we don't think about other people's feelings. We all do wrong things every day, but if we say sorry to Jesus, he forgives us and we can start again.

Confession

Lord Jesus, we are sorry that we sometimes don't do what you want. We want to start again, like Matthew. Please help us to learn how to do what you want. Amen.

Song

I'm special (KS: 162)

Activity

Play a game of 'Follow the leader' or 'Simon says'.

Talk outline

When we played that game, we all tried to do as we were told. It's like that with Jesus. There are things he says we should do, especially the things written down in the Bible. We're not very good at following what he says, just as we might not have been very good at following what *(insert name of leader)* said in that game. But, because we are Jesus' friends, we want to try.

Alternative activity

'Follow Me!' on page 69 of *100 Worship Activities for Children*.

Prayers

Father God, please help us to know that it's wrong when we try to cheat others. Help us to follow Jesus instead. Amen.

Final song

There is power in the name of Jesus (KS: 326)

Launchpad song is played as the congregation leave.

Matthew meets Jesus

Cast
Narrators 1 and 2 (positioned on either side of stage)
Taxpayers (one of whom hobbles)
Soldier (in biblical costume)
Matthew (in biblical costume)
Jesus (in biblical costume)

Props
Table, with sign saying 'Matthew's tax office', and chair
Second table, with simple food and two chairs
Bags of money or piles of bank notes

Taxpayers line up at first table, grumbling. Soldier stands guard.

NARRATOR 1: Here's a man who Jesus met…
NARRATOR 2: Matthew was his name.

Enter Matthew. He walks to table and sits.

NARRATOR 1: He wasn't very popular…

Taxpayers grumble louder, and start booing.

NARRATOR 2: But guess what he became!

Taxpayers hand money over in turn.

NARRATOR 1: He was Jewish, but his job…
NARRATOR 2: Meant Jews paid him tax.

Matthew begins to count the pile of money.

NARRATOR 1: He gave most to the Romans, but…
NARRATOR 2: Kept some behind their backs.

As taxpayers walk away, Matthew pockets some of the money.

NARRATOR 1: He got rich as they got poor…
NARRATOR 2: They thought it was unfair.

One taxpayer sees what Matthew's doing and shows others. They approach Matthew threateningly.

NARRATOR 1: But if they made a fuss at all…
NARRATOR 2: Roman soldiers would be there.

Soldier steps in. Matthew pulls face at them. Enter Jesus.

NARRATOR 1: When Jesus came to town that day…

NARRATOR 2: People were impressed.

Taxpayers turn to look at Jesus.

NARRATOR 1: He healed the sick and taught them well…

NARRATOR 2: About who would be blessed.

Jesus rests a hand on the hobbling taxpayer. He leaps and shouts as if healed. Others look impressed.

NARRATOR 1: Matthew thought he'd like to see…

NARRATOR 2: This amazing preacher guy.

Matthew sits at his desk, counting money, feeling shy about approaching Jesus.

NARRATOR 1: But he thought he was no good…

NARRATOR 2: And Jesus would walk on by.

NARRATOR 1: Yet as he sat there in his place…

Jesus approaches Matthew's table.

NARRATOR 2: He saw his hero pause…

Jesus points at Matthew.

NARRATOR 1: Point at him… say, 'Come with me'.

Taxpayers start laughing.

NARRATOR 2: Ignoring the guffaws…

Matthew stands.

NARRATOR 1: Matthew stood and realized…

NARRATOR 2: This meant: 'Be my friend.'

Matthew approaches Jesus, who shakes his hand warmly.

NARRATOR 1: It was his chance to start again…

NARRATOR 2: Escape from his dead end.

NARRATOR 1: He left his table and his tax…

Matthew and Jesus walk away from table, deep in conversation.

NARRATOR 2: His life changed in a flash…

NARRATOR 1: He was now Jesus' friend…

NARRATOR 2: No more collecting cash.

Matthew throws money into air. Taxpayers look at each other, then scrabble around on floor, picking up money.

NARRATOR 1: Jesus came to Matthew's house…

Jesus and Matthew reach other side of stage, and sit down. They chat.

NARRATOR 2: To have a proper dinner.

NARRATOR 1: When people saw where Jesus was…

Taxpayers notice Jesus and nudge each other. They point indignantly.

NARRATOR 2: They said, 'He's with a sinner!'

Matthew stands and mimes talking to them..

NARRATOR 1: But Matthew said, 'This special man…

NARRATOR 2: Wanted to come and meet me.

NARRATOR 1: That's amazing! I know now…

NARRATOR 2: He'll change my life completely.'

Reproduced with permission from *Launchpad* published by BRF 2004 (1 84101 326 9)

Peter: Jesus' crucifixion

 Teaching point

Jesus can forgive us when we do things we know are wrong.

 Bible passages

Luke 22:54–62; John 21:15–19; 1 John 2:2

 Key verse

Christ is the sacrifice that takes away our sins and the sins of all the world's people.

1 JOHN 2:2

 Visual aids

None needed

SERVICE FRAMEWORK

★ **Welcome the congregation.** ★

Song

Sing the *Launchpad* song.

Talk outline

 Recap the story of Matthew. We're meeting another of Jesus' friends today. He's called Peter and he worked as a fisherman. But Jesus also said to him, 'Stop what you're doing and follow me.'

Song

One man was Peter (The Big Book of Spring Harvest Kids' Praise: 100)

Optional sketch: The weaker link

See www.launchpad-services.com for script.

Talk outline

 Sometimes we let our friends down. That's what happened to Peter. He let Jesus down.

Drama

Peter meets Jesus *(see pages 90–91 for script)*.

Alternative activity

 'The Crucifixion', focusing on Peter's worry monster, from pages 42–43 of *Worship!*

Talk outline

 How did Peter let Jesus down? Do you think Jesus was upset? Sometimes we let Jesus down as well. Can you think of ways we let Jesus down? We'll use your ideas for our prayers later.

Song

Everybody has a wobble (KS: 46)

Activity

 'Demolition' from page 127 or 'Caught Red-Handed' from page 130 of *100 Worship Activities for Children*. Alternatively, read the crucifixion story using 'Story cubes' described on pages 91–92 of *The Road to Easter*.

Confession

Ask members of the congregation for suggestions about the ways we let Jesus down. Write them on OHP or flipchart, and pray for forgiveness.

Song

I believe in Jesus (KS: 122)

Talk outline

 The good news is that Peter and Jesus made friends with each other again. After Jesus died and came back to life, this is how it happened.

Reading

Read John 21:15–19.

Talk outline

 Recap the story from the reading, explaining that Jesus forgave Peter for letting him down and gave him an important job. We've learnt that we all let Jesus down, just like Peter. The good news is Jesus loves us, died for us and wants to forgive us. He helps us make a new start. So when you do things wrong this week, say sorry to Jesus and ask him to help you start again.

Final song

From heaven you came (KS: 62)

The *Launchpad* song is played as the congregation leaves.

Peter meets Jesus

NARRATOR 1: Here's a man who Jesus met…
NARRATOR 2: Peter was his name.

Enter Peter.

NARRATOR 1: He wasn't too intelligent…

Peter trips over his own feet and nearly falls.

NARRATOR 2: But guess what he became!
NARRATOR 1: He loved fishing, and his job…
NARRATOR 2: Meant he lived by the sea.

Peter sits and mimes casting out fishing-net. Enter Jesus, with disciples.

NARRATOR 1: His fishing stopped when Jesus came…
NARRATOR 2: And told him, 'Follow me.'

Jesus points at Peter and then motions for him to follow.

NARRATOR 1: He went with Jesus for three years…

Peter joins other disciples and shakes hands eagerly.

NARRATOR 2: Saw miracles and healing.

Jesus pours water from one glass into another which contains a small amount of red food colouring. The water appears to turn into wine. Disciples and Peter gasp.

NARRATOR 1: Heard great stories, learnt a lot…
NARRATOR 2: It was a happy feeling.

Jesus teaches disciples.

NARRATOR 1: Peter wasn't clever, so…

 Cast
Narrators 1 and 2
Peter *(in biblical costume)*
Disciples *(in biblical costume)*
Jesus *(in biblical costume)*
Soldiers *(in biblical costume)*
Crowd 1 and Crowd 2 *(in biblical costume)*

 Props
Water
Two glasses
Red food colouring

 Sound effects
Cock crowing

Reproduced with permission from *Launchpad* published by BRF 2004 (1 84101 326 9)

Peter raises his hand eagerly.

NARRATOR 2: Kept getting things all wrong.

Jesus shakes his head gently. Peter looks downcast.

NARRATOR 1: But he made friends who didn't mind…
NARRATOR 2: Their group seemed really strong.

Other disciples pat Peter on the back or make expressions suggesting that it doesn't matter. Other disciples leave.

NARRATOR 1: Peter thought, 'We're friends for life!'

Peter and Jesus shake hands.

NARRATOR 2: But Jesus gave this warning…

Jesus points at Peter and mimes speaking.

NARRATOR 1: 'Peter,' he said, 'you'll let me down…
NARRATOR 2: Three times before the morning.'

Peter looks horrified and wags finger.

NARRATOR 1: 'No way!' said Peter, but that night…
NARRATOR 2: He saw Jesus arrested.

Soldier enters, and grabs Jesus.

NARRATOR 1: Some people thought he was a threat…
NARRATOR 2: They wanted his claims tested.

Soldier drags Jesus off.

NARRATOR 1: The group of friends that Peter had…
NARRATOR 2: Disappeared quite quickly.

Peter looks around and realizes he is alone.

NARRATOR 1: He found himself alone that night…
NARRATOR 2: And feeling rather sickly.

Enter crowd 1 and crowd 2.

NARRATOR 1: When people said, 'You're Jesus' friend!'

Crowd 1 points at Peter.

NARRATOR 2: He was scared. He thought he'd die.
NARRATOR 1: He said he didn't know the man…

Peter shakes his head. Crowd 2 points. Peter shakes his head again.

NARRATOR 2: Three times he told that lie.
NARRATOR 1: Then a cock crowed. *(FX: cock crowing)* It was dawn.
NARRATOR 2: What Jesus said came true.

Peter looks horrified.

NARRATOR 1: He had let his good friend down.

Peter cries.

NARRATOR 2: He cried. Well, wouldn't you?
NARRATOR 1: Just like us, he did things wrong…
NARRATOR 2: However hard he tried.

Soldier brings Jesus on. Jesus looks at Peter with sadness but compassion.

NARRATOR 1: Jesus knows it's difficult…
NARRATOR 2: That's why he was crucified.

Soldier mimes banging nails into Jesus' hands. Peter kneels at foot of cross.

NARRATOR 1: Peter said, 'He died for me!
NARRATOR 2: Why he did defeats me.
NARRATOR 1: He's amazing! I know now…
NARRATOR 2: He's changed my life completely.'

Reproduced with permission from *Launchpad* published by BRF 2004 (1 84101 326 9)

Mary: Jesus' resurrection

 Teaching point

Are we excited enough by Jesus' resurrection to want to tell others?

 Bible passages

John 20:11–18; Matthew 28:16–20

 Key verse

Go to the people of all nations and make them my disciples.

MATTHEW 28:19

 Visual aids

Stickers with the words 'Ask me about my good news!' *(see template on page 93 or download from www.launchpad-services.com)*

Sweets *(to be given out at the end of the service)*

SERVICE FRAMEWORK

★ ★

Welcome the congregation.

★ ★

Song

Sing the *Launchpad* song.

Talk outline

 Recap the stories of Matthew and Peter. Mary's life changed even more when she met Jesus. She had been unfaithful to her husband. Everyone thought she was a bad lot, but Jesus didn't condemn her. What did we hear about Jesus in the last *Launchpad*? Mary was very sad when Jesus died. She went to his burial place because she wanted to remember him.

Drama

Mary meets Jesus *(see pages 94–95 for script)*.

Talk outline

 Mary discovered that Jesus was alive! He had died, but he had come back to life. That was really important. It meant that Jesus really was who he said he was. That was really exciting for her. It's exciting news for us too.

Song

Led like a lamb (SOF: 322) or
The women went to Jesus' tomb (KS: 337)

Talk outline

Mary was so excited that she ran back to tell Jesus' other friends about what had happened. They weren't as excited because they didn't believe her at first.

Optional sketch: Big Sister

See www.launchpad-services.com for script.

Activity

Select a child to go out of the worship area with a *Launchpad* leader who tells him or her quietly that there are sweets for all the children after the service. When you have good news, it's difficult to keep it secret. You want to tell everyone.

Say, 'We're going to tell *(insert name of child)* some good news. Can they can keep it secret?'

When the child returns, say, 'Have you got some good news for everyone?' *(The service leader persuades the child to share it.)* 'That was good news. But the good news that Jesus is alive is worth shouting about even more.'

Ask me about my good news!

Alternative activity

 'Easter' from pages 22–23 of *Worship!*

Song

God's not dead (KS: 85)

Reading

Read Matthew 28:16–20.

Talk outline

 Recap the story from the reading. Jesus said that he would always be with us. His followers, like Mary, were so excited that Jesus is alive that they had to tell people all about it. That's how the Church started. Jesus asks us to do the same. When we are out and about—at work or school, playing football or going to see our friends—perhaps we too could tell others that Jesus is alive.

Prayers

Ask God to help us tell our friends the good news about Jesus. See prayers on page 67 of *Worship through the Christian Year: Year A* for examples.

Talk outline

 To help us tell our friends about Jesus, we've produced some stickers. They read, 'Ask me about my good news!' If you wear this sticker, people will ask you about it. What will you tell them?

Final hymn

Tell out my soul (SOF: 520) or
Jesus, we celebrate your victory (KS: 217)

The *Launchpad* song is played as the congregation leaves. Stickers reading 'Ask me about my good news!' and sweets are given out as everyone leaves.

Mary meets Jesus

 Cast
Narrators 1 and 2
Mary *(in biblical costume)*
Pharisees *(in biblical costume)*
Jesus *(in biblical costume)*
Soldier *(in biblical costume)*
Friends and disciples *(in biblical costume)*

 Props
Boxes denoting spices and perfume

NARRATOR 1: Here's a woman Jesus met…
NARRATOR 2: Mary was her name.

Enter Mary.

NARRATOR 1: She wasn't great at being good.
NARRATOR 2: But guess what she became!

Enter Jesus and Pharisees.

NARRATOR 1: Pharisees caught her doing wrong…

Pharisees grab her and throw her at the feet of Jesus.

NARRATOR 2: They said she should be dead.

Pharisees point and mime picking up stones.

NARRATOR 1: But Jesus said, 'You throw your stones…
NARRATOR 2: If you're perfect instead.'

Pharisees freeze.

NARRATOR 1: No one moved. So Jesus said…

Pharisees mime dropping stones and exit.

NARRATOR 2: 'Why don't you follow me?'

Jesus beckons to Mary.

NARRATOR 1: Mary did, and learnt from him…
NARRATOR 2: How she should really be.

Enter soldier.

NARRATOR 1: The day that Jesus died, she thought…

Reproduced with permission from *Launchpad* published by BRF 2004 (1 84101 326 9)

Soldier mimes nailing Jesus to cross, as in script for previous Launchpad.

NARRATOR 2: 'My life won't be the same.
NARRATOR 1: This man helped me change my life…
NARRATOR 2: I'll have to start again.'

Soldier carries Jesus' body off.

NARRATOR 1: She was so sad, she found some friends…

Friends enter, carrying spices and perfume.

NARRATOR 2: And visited his grave…

Mary and friends comfort each other.

NARRATOR 1: To pay respects to Jesus, who'd…
NARRATOR 2: Taught them how to behave.
NARRATOR 1: Early Sunday, off they went…

Mary and friends go to one side of stage.

NARRATOR 2: With oil, perfume and spices.
NARRATOR 1: But they found the body gone…

Mary and friends mime looking in the grave, and are shocked.

NARRATOR 2: It was a real crisis!
NARRATOR 1: The others went, but Mary stayed…

Exit friends.

NARRATOR 2: She was crying, and so shaken.

Mary cries. Enter Jesus.

NARRATOR 1: A man said, 'Hey, what's wrong with you?'

Jesus mimes asking her the question.

NARRATOR 2: She said, 'Where's he been taken?'

NARRATOR 1: She thought it was the gardener, but…
NARRATOR 2: Just then he said her name.
NARRATOR 1: 'Mary!' said Jesus. Then she knew…

Jesus mouths 'Mary'. Mary looks up and recognizes him.

NARRATOR 2: He'd come to life again.
NARRATOR 1: 'Teacher!' she cried. 'You are alive!
NARRATOR 2: I just don't know how!'

Mary goes to hug him, but he stops her.

NARRATOR 1: Then Jesus said, 'Tell all my friends…
NARRATOR 2: That you have seen me now.'

Jesus smiles and sends her away.

NARRATOR 1: Mary ran to the disciples' house…
NARRATOR 2: As fast as she could go.

Mary runs to other side of stage and meets disciples. Exit Jesus.

NARRATOR 1: She had good news to tell them all…
NARRATOR 2: Some news they ought to know.
NARRATOR 1: She told them, 'Jesus rose again…

Mary mimes speaking animatedly.

NARRATOR 2: And then he came to meet me.
NARRATOR 1: That's amazing! I know now…
NARRATOR 2: He's changed my life completely.'

LAUNCHPAD TV

This series uses 'TV programmes' to teach the significance of the gifts brought by the magi. The programmes include a soap opera, news (about world issues), quiz and Bible story. There are opportunities for worship (called 'Praise TV') and prayer ('Feedback'). An announcer introduces each programme and draws out the teaching points. The series is ideal for Advent, Christmas or Epiphany or even for a Christmas holiday club.

Each programme's title appears on the OHP screen as a signature tune is played. Download ready-made PowerPoint presentations from www.launchpad-services.com. Create signature tunes for each programme or use music from other sources.

The issues studied and relevant Bible passages are:

1. Gold (Matthew 13:44; Job 22:25): What is the most precious thing in your life?

2. Frankincense (Deuteronomy 6:5; 2 Corinthians 2:15): Jesus is God. True worship is like a fragrant offering to him.

3. Myrrh (Isaiah 53:5; John 3:16): Jesus was born to save us. He had to die to do so.

The Bible passages are put together as part of the quiz show.

Gold

 Teaching point

What is the most precious thing in your life?

 Bible passages

Matthew 13:44; Job 22:25.

 Key verse

The kingdom of heaven is like… treasure hidden in a field.

MATTHEW 13:44

 Visual aids

A box painted gold and giftwrapped

Three glasses of water—one fresh, one salty and one 'dirty' *(see 'Newshound' on page 99)*

Cards with right and wrong answers *(for use in 'Runabout!' on page 100)*

Bible verse cards *(photocopied from template on page 104)*

SERVICE FRAMEWORK

★★★★★★★★★★★★★★★★★★★★★★★★★★★★
★   ★
★   **Welcome the congregation.**   ★
★   ★
★★★★★★★★★★★★★★★★★★★★★★★★★★★★

Song

Sing the *Launchpad* song. (The congregation may have to learn it first.)

Talk outline

 Beforehand, paint a box gold and giftwrap it. Introduce the format and theme: we're looking at the presents the magi brought to Jesus. Ask a child to unwrap the first gift, describe it as a gold bar and display it at the front. Explain that gold is a precious metal. It shows Jesus was born to be king. We'll be exploring things that are precious to us. God should be the most precious of all.

Arty fax

 Visit children's Sunday groups beforehand and ask them to draw something precious to them. Judge a winner in each age group. Incorporate the winning drawings into your PowerPoint presentation or acetates. All the children's work could be displayed around the church.

Before viewing the winning drawings, show a reproduction of the Wilton Diptych. (Find it at www.nationalgallery.org.uk.) Explain that the gold leaf is not the most precious part of it. The ultramarine blue, made from precious stones called lapis lazuli, was more valuable.

Show the winning drawings, ask the artists about them and give them prizes.

Talk outline

 We all think different things are precious. Sometimes the most precious thing is not what we think it is.

Praise TV

Lord, you are more precious than silver (SOF 368) or Lord, you are so precious to me (SOF 369)

Drama

Soap Street 1 *(see pages 101–103 for script).*

Talk outline

 We are precious to God. When we turn away from God, it's as if we are lost, but Jesus finds us and brings us back. Thanks to Jesus, we are found. Heaven celebrates when we turn back to God.

Feedback

Rehearse the response beforehand.

Leader: God of all good things, you give us all we need, but sometimes we want things that are bad for us. We think we need them, but we don't really. Sometimes we behave badly if we don't get those things. Precious Father…

All: **Forgive us and help us to put you first.**

Leader: God of all creation, we have so much when others have so little. We waste things that are rare and precious in other places. When we forget about people around the world and treat your creation badly, precious Father…

All: **Forgive us and help us to put you first.**

Leader: God of all, we are so precious to you that you sent your Son to bring us back to you. Thank you that you gave the most precious gift ever. Sometimes we look in the wrong places for something to treasure. When we are dazzled by the glint of gold and miss the baby in a manger, precious Father…

All: **Forgive us and help us to put you first.**

Leader: Holy God, when we really are sorry, you forgive us. Show us your mercy, change our hearts and help us to keep you number one in our lives.

All: **Amen.**

Storybook

Invite the youngest children to gather around. Read the story of Zacchaeus from Luke 19:1–10. Alternatively, use 'The Magpie's Tale' from *Animal Tales*. Ask the publishers if you can display the illustrations and show them on an OHP screen as you tell the story.

Talk outline

 Zacchaeus thought money was precious, but he found that knowing Jesus is better. Like Zacchaeus, we're precious to God. He gave Jesus to save us.

Praise TV

Nobody liked Zacchaeus (KS: 261) or
I'm special (KS: 162)

Newshound

 Newshound could be dressed as a dog or a reporter. Have three glasses of water (one fresh, one salty and one 'dirty') and cups for the children. Simulate dirty water by adding gravy powder and dried herbs to tap water.

Newshound reveals statistics about water (for example, two-thirds of the planet is covered by water, but only three per cent is fresh water). He tastes the salty water and offers it to the children. It's horrible! Explain that not all fresh water is drinkable. He tastes the 'dirty' water and offers it to the children. It's horrible! Explain how precious fresh water is. For more information, visit the Tearfund website at www.tearfund.org.

Praise TV

As the deer pants for the water (SOF: 27)

Runabout!

 For each question, the announcer's assistants hold up cards, each showing one of two possible answers. The announcer asks a question and shouts 'Go!' The children run to the card showing what they think is the correct answer. They can then change their minds as the host shouts 'Runabout

now!' Once they've made their final decision, reveal the answer. Children who get it wrong are out. At the end of the quiz, the remaining children split into two teams. Each is given fragments of a different key Bible verse. They race to rearrange the words, each helped by an assistant. Prizes are awarded, and the congregation learns both verses.

1: **What is used to make ultramarine blue?**
   Correct: lapis lazuli
   Wrong: gold

2: **Where was Bobby's football found?**
   Correct: in the church garden
   Wrong: in the launderette

3: **What did Zacchaeus climb to see Jesus?**
   Correct: a tree
   Wrong: a ladder

4: **What covers two-thirds of our planet?**
   Correct: water
   Wrong: grass

 Key verses
The kingdom of heaven is like... treasure hidden in a field.
MATTHEW 13:44

Let God All-Powerful be your silver and gold.
JOB 22:25

Feedback

Father God, thank you that we know we're precious to you. You love us so much that you sent your Son. Help those who don't know how precious you are to find out. Amen.

Praise TV

We three kings (from *Carols for Children*)

Launchpad song plays as congregation leaves.

Soap Street 1

 Cast
Schoolboy Bobby
Bobby's friend Mickey
Bobby's mum Sheryl
Schoolgirl Katie
Katie's dad Jim

 Props
Cardboard boxes with holes cut in front to
denote washing machines in launderette
Counter
Stuffed toy dog
Full laundry bag
Football covered in signatures

 **Sound effects**
Theme tune

Play theme tune. Sheryl is standing at the counter filing her nails. Enter Bobby and Mickey looking for something.

BOBBY:	All right, Mum?
SHERYL:	All right? Is that any way to talk to your mother?
MICKEY:	All right, Mrs Watson?

Sheryl rolls her eyes, despairingly.

SHERYL:	Have you done the shopping yet, Bobby?
BOBBY:	Sorry, Mum. Too busy. We're looking for Vindaloo.
SHERYL:	You should be looking in an Indian restaurant, then—not a launderette!
BOBBY:	Vindaloo's his dog! I was showing Mickey my football when the stupid dog grabbed it and ran off!

SHERYL:	Can't you just buy another one, Bobby? They don't cost that much.
BOBBY:	It's the one signed by all the City players, Mum.
SHERYL:	What? Not the one signed by the team that won the cup? That's priceless!
BOBBY:	Yeah. It's my bestest thing in the world ever!
SHERYL:	What would Mickey's dog want with it? He wouldn't bring it here, surely?
MICKEY:	No. Bobby just came to tell you he can't go shopping.
BOBBY:	Yeah, only 'cos of your stupid dog.
MICKEY:	Vindaloo isn't stupid. He's dead clever!
SHERYL:	What sort of a name is Vindaloo anyway?
MICKEY:	It's because he'll only eat curry!

Enter Katie with laundry bag.

KATIE:	Good morning.
SHERYL:	Morning, love. There you go, Bobby—a nice young lady with proper manners. *(To Katie)* Haven't seen you in here before, have we?
KATIE:	No. I'm Katie. *(Offering a hand for Sheryl to shake. Sheryl takes it)*
SHERYL:	Nice to meet you, Katie. What can I do for you?
KATIE:	Can I get these dry-cleaned, please? *(Hands bag to Sheryl)*
SHERYL:	Of course, love. *(Exits with bag)*
MICKEY:	*(To Katie)* You haven't seen Vindaloo, have you?
KATIE:	Sorry?
MICKEY:	My dog, Vindaloo. He's run off.
BOBBY:	Yeah, with my football. It's signed by all those City players!
KATIE:	Wow! I'd love to see that!
BOBBY:	Well, if I ever find it again, I'll show you.
KATIE:	Well, I lost my City scarf once and I was really worried.
MICKEY:	You're a City fan? Cool!
BOBBY:	So what did you do?
KATIE:	Well, I looked everywhere and couldn't find it. *(Embarrassed)* So I thought maybe I should pray about it.

MICKEY:	Pray?
KATIE:	Yeah. Sounds funny, I know. But it turned up straight away.
BOBBY:	Really? Do you think it might work for me?
MICKEY:	You are joking, Bobby!
KATIE:	It can't do any harm.
BOBBY:	I'll give anything a go. What do I do, Katie?
KATIE:	Just talk to God like you're talking to me.
BOBBY:	OK, here goes… *(Looking up at the ceiling)* Er, hello God. I don't normally do this, but I need your help. My bestest thing in the world ever is missing and I don't know what to do. Please help me find it. Er… that's it.
KATIE:	Amen.

Enter Jim, carrying stuffed toy dog and signed football.

KATIE:	Hello, Dad!
MICKEY:	Vindaloo! *(Grabs dog and strokes him furiously)* Where have you been, boy?
JIM:	I found him digging in the church garden. He was trying to bury this. *(Holds up football)*
BOBBY:	My football!

Enter Sheryl.

BOBBY:	Look, Mum, Katie's dad found it!
SHERYL:	That's great news! Now you can do my shopping! *(Bobby's face falls)*
KATIE:	Hey, Bobby. Did you see? God answered your prayer!
BOBBY:	Yeah!
KATIE:	You might want to say thank you.
BOBBY:	How do I do that?
JIM:	Well, why don't you go to church with Katie tomorrow?

BOBBY:	Er… I don't know. I've never been before. What do you reckon, Mickey?
MICKEY:	No way. I'm not going to church!
SHERYL:	I'll come with you, Bobby. What time's the service?
JIM:	Half-past ten.
MICKEY:	You're not really going to go to church are you, mate?
BOBBY:	Why not? I prayed for God to help me and he did.
KATIE:	That might be just the beginning.
JIM:	You might find something even more precious…

All freeze. Theme music to end.

Reproduced with permission from *Launchpad* published by BRF 2004 (1 84101 326 9)

The kingdom of heaven is like… treasure hidden in a field.

MATTHEW 13:44

Let God All-Powerful be your silver and gold.

JOB 22:25

Frankincense

Teaching point

Jesus is God. True worship is like a fragrant offering to him.

Bible passages

Deuteronomy 6:5; 2 Corinthians 2:15.

Key verse

Your life must be controlled by love, just as Christ loved us and gave his life for us as a sweet-smelling offering... that pleases God.

EPHESIANS 5:2 (GNB)

Visual aids

Gold box used in the previous *Launchpad* TV service

Bottle of perfume *(giftwrapped)*

Cards with right and wrong answers *(for use in 'Runabout!' on pages 106–107)*

Bible verse cards *(photocopied from template on page 110)*

SERVICE FRAMEWORK

★★★★★★★★★★★★★★★★★★★★★★★★★★★
★   ★
★   **Welcome the congregation.**   ★
★   ★
★★★★★★★★★★★★★★★★★★★★★★★★★★★

Song

Sing the *Launchpad* song.

Talk outline

Beforehand, giftwrap a bottle of perfume. Display the gold box, unwrapped. Recap the theme and ask a child to unwrap the second gift and display it at the front. Explain that frankincense is a kind of perfume used in worship. The smell reminds us that Jesus is God come to live among us. Like the sweet smell of perfume, his life pleased God. Ours can, too.

On your marks, get set, cook!

Visit children's Sunday groups beforehand. Ask them to think of food that smells unpleasant and food that smells pleasant. Nominate two children to take part in *Launchpad*. Give one child three items that smell unpleasant, and the other child three that smell pleasant.

Provide two tables, mixing-bowls and wooden spoons. Introduce each child, and ask what they've brought. Give each one 30 seconds to mix their three ingredients. Smell each concoction. Exaggerate the unpleasant smell of one and the pleasant smell of the other. Offer the bowls to the congregation to smell.

Unpleasant smells could include fish paste, garlic powder and vinegar. Pleasant smells could include chocolate spread, toffee sauce and honey.

Talk outline

The Bible says that our lives and worship are like a smell to God. Jesus' life was like a lovely perfume to God. Ours can be, too. If we do wrong things, our lives are like an unpleasant smell.

Praise TV

May the fragrance of Jesus fill this place (SOF: 388)

Drama

Soap Street 2 *(see pages 108–109 for script)*.

Talk outline

 We should worship God. Anything we put first in our lives instead of God will let us down.

Feedback

Rehearse the response beforehand.

Leader: God of the universe, when we think about your creation, from the vastness of space to the intricacy of atoms, we are amazed. Yet so often we forget about you and live as if you weren't there. God with us…

All: **Forgive us and help us to worship you.**

Leader: God our Father, you have made us your children. You always want the best for us, but so often we think we know better and ignore you. The wrong things we think, say and do make you sad. God with us…

All: **Forgive us and help us to worship you.**

Leader: God of the stable, you come so close to us. You long to spend time with us, but so often we busy ourselves with other things. We miss your voice whispering your love in our hearts. God with us…

All: **Forgive us and help us to worship you.**

Leader: Holy God, when we really are sorry, you forgive us. Show us your mercy, change our hearts and help us to worship you in our lives.

All: **Amen.**

Storybook

Read the story of Jesus calming the storm from Mark 4:35–41. Alternatively, use 'The Mouse's Tale' from *Animal Tales*.

Talk outline

 Because Jesus calmed the storm, his disciples began to understand that he was God. In the end, they realized that they should worship him. So should we.

Praise TV

He walked where I walk (SOF: 172)

Newshound

Newshound explains how we are free to worship God. It's not like that everywhere. In some countries, telling others about Jesus is against the law. Use material from Christian Solidarity Worldwide (www.csw.org.uk) or Release International (www.releaseinternational.org) to illustrate.

Praise TV

We shall stand with our feet on the rock (SOF: 589) or Lord, the light of your love is shining (KS: 237)

Runabout!

 As before, for each question, the announcer's assistants hold up cards, each showing one of two possible answers. The announcer asks a

question and shouts 'Go!' The children run to the card showing what they think is the correct answer. They can then change their minds as the host shouts 'Runabout now!' Once they've made their final decision, reveal the answer. Children who get it wrong are out. At the end of the quiz, the remaining children split into two teams.

Each is given fragments of a different Bible verse. They race to rearrange the words, each helped by an assistant. Prizes are awarded, and the congregation learns both verses.

1: **Who mixed food that smelt unpleasant?**
Correct: *(insert name)*
Wrong: *(insert name)*

2: **Where did Bobby go on Sunday morning in Soap Street?**
Correct: To the cup final
Wrong: To church

3: **Who was asleep in the boat during the storm?**
Correct: Jesus
Wrong: Peter

4: **In which countries is it against the law to tell people about Jesus?**
Correct: *(insert name of country)*
Wrong: Britain

Key verse
Love the Lord your God with all your heart, soul, and strength.
DEUTERONOMY 6:5

Your life must be controlled by love, just as Christ loved us and gave his life for us as a sweet-smelling offering... that pleases God.
EPHESIANS 5:2 (GNB)

Feedback

Father God, thank you that we're free to worship you and tell people about Jesus. Help those in other countries who get into trouble for doing what you say. Amen.

Praise TV

We three kings (from *Carols for Children*)

Launchpad song plays as congregation leaves.

Soap Street 2

 Cast
Bobby
Sheryl
Mickey
Katie

 Props
Sofa
Two computer game console controllers
Telephone

Sound effects
Theme tune
Doorbell ring
Games console

Play theme music. Bobby is on the sofa playing computer games. Doorbell rings. Bobby looks at door and peers in other direction.

BOBBY: *(Shouts)* Mu-u-m, door!

Sheryl enters, stops behind sofa, looks at Bobby, puts her hands on her hips and shakes her head. Doorbell rings again.

BOBBY: *(Shouts louder, unaware that Sheryl is behind him)* MU-U-M!
SHERYL: I can hear you! *(Bobby jumps in fright)* Get the door yourself, couch potato!

Bobby reluctantly gets up and opens imaginary door. Sheryl exits. Mickey enters.

MICKEY: All right, mate?
BOBBY: *(Sits back on sofa. Continues playing computer game)* All right, Mickey!
MICKEY: Still can't believe we're playing United in the cup final.
BOBBY: Fantastic if you've got cable!
MICKEY: Or tickets.
BOBBY: Yeah! But we ain't got neither, so what's the point?

Mickey comes to sit next to Bobby and slumps into sofa. Pulls two tickets from pocket and waves them about.

BOBBY::   No way! Are those…?
MICKEY: Yeah! Two tickets to see City play United tomorrow!
BOBBY: You're joking! *(Grabs tickets)* How did you get them?
MICKEY: My dad. He got three. One for me, one for him and… one for you!

BOBBY: You're the bestest mate ever!

They march around, chanting 'City!' Sheryl enters. Bobby suddenly stops. Mickey bumps into him and they fall over.

SHERYL: What are you two up to?
BOBBY: Mickey's got me a ticket for the cup final.
SHERYL: *(Disappointed)* You wanted to go to church tomorrow.
BOBBY: *(Feigning remorse)* Sorry, Mum. Can I go to the football, please? Mickey's dad's going.
SHERYL: I suppose so. *(Bobby hugs her)* All right. Get off before I change my mind.

Sheryl exits.

BOBBY: Cool! This is the bestest thing in the world ever!
MICKEY: Better than going to church?
BOBBY: Miles!
MICKEY: You don't want to say no more prayers, then?
BOBBY: Nah! City won't let us down!

Bobby and Mickey exit.

Indicate that it is the next day. Enter Bobby, looking sad. He slumps on to sofa, fiddles half-heartedly with games console controller. Doorbell rings. Bobby ignores it. It rings again. Bobby looks at door and peers in other direction.

BOBBY: *(Calls, half-heartedly)* Mu-u-m, door!

Doorbell rings again, Bobby opens mouth to shout again, but decides to open it himself. Katie enters.

BOBBY: *(Sadly)* All right, Katie?
KATIE: Hi, Bobby. Can you believe that third goal? It was definitely offside.
BOBBY: *(Shuts door and wanders back to sofa)* Yeah.
KATIE: *(Sits next to him)* Didn't see you and your mum at church today. Did you see the match here?
BOBBY: No. Me and Mickey had tickets. Needn't have bothered, though. City had a nightmare. I really wanted to see them winning the cup.
KATIE: It's really important to you, isn't it?
BOBBY: They let me down, though, didn't they?
KATIE: This morning at church, they said Jesus never lets us down.
BOBBY: Really? Maybe I should support him.
KATIE: That would be fantastic!
BOBBY: But can I support Jesus and City?
KATIE: Of course.
BOBBY: I'm sorry I didn't come to church.
KATIE: That's OK. But you would have really liked it this week.
BOBBY: How come?
KATIE: They had a big screen set up in the hall. We all watched the match after the service.

Bobby pulls a face. They freeze. Theme music to end.

Reproduced with permission from *Launchpad* published by BRF 2004 (1 84101 326 9)

Love the Lord your God
with all your heart, soul
and strength.

DEUTERONOMY 6:5

Your life must be controlled
by love, just as Christ loved
us and gave his life for us as
a sweet-smelling offering…
that pleases God.

EPHESIANS 5:2 (GNB)

Myrrh

SERVICE FRAMEWORK

★ ★
★   ★
★   **Welcome the congregation.**   ★
★   ★
★ ★

Song

Sing the *Launchpad* song.

Talk outline

Before the service, giftwrap a small pot of cream or embalming fluid.

Display the gold and frankincense, un-wrapped. Recap the theme and ask a child to unwrap the third gift and display it at the front. Explain that, unlike gold and frankincense, this isn't the kind of gift you'd like. Embalming fluid is used to prepare a dead body for burial. Myrrh was used in Jesus' time in the same way. This gift reminds us that Jesus came with a mission. To complete that mission, he had to die.

Make-it challenge

Visit children's Sunday groups beforehand. Each child makes a model nativity scene. (Download a template from www.launchpad-services.com.)

Invite two adults to do the same in *Launchpad*, but deprive them of the necessary tools (for example, scissors and tape), give them incomprehensible instructions (for example, in a foreign language) and don't give enough time (for example, only 30 seconds). The resulting models will be incomplete. Point out that the children have made the models correctly, and display the best examples.

Talk outline

The children had the right materials, good instructions and someone to help. When we do it on our own, the result is a mess. Our lives are the same. God sent Jesus to sort out our mess. If we follow his instructions, he shows us what to do.

Praise TV

Don't build your house on the sandy land (KS: 40)

Drama

Soap Street 3 (see pages 114–115 for script).

Talk outline

 Just like Katie paid for Bobby's mistake, Jesus has paid the price for us on the cross.

Feedback

Rehearse the response beforehand.

Leader:	God of all goodness, you showed us the way to live in your Son, Jesus. Sometimes we don't follow the right way. We hurt you and others through the things we forget to do. God, our Saviour…
All:	**Forgive us and give us your grace.**
Leader:	God of all strength, you give us your Holy Spirit to help us follow Jesus. Sometimes we don't rely on your strength and find it hard to resist temptation. God, our Saviour…
All:	**Forgive us and give us your grace.**
Leader:	God of all love, you gave your Son to die to save us. Sometimes we choose to think, say or do wrong things. God, our Saviour…
All:	**Forgive us and give us your grace.**
Leader:	Holy God, when we really are sorry, you forgive us. Show us your mercy, change our hearts and give us your grace to live as you want.
All:	**Amen.**

Storybook

Read the story of the shepherds visiting Jesus from Luke 2:8–20, or use 'The Fox's Tale' in *Animal Tales*.

Talk outline

 Shepherds were regarded as the lowest of the low in Jesus' day and nobody wanted them around. They might have thought they weren't important to anyone, but God chose to send his message to them first. They were the first people to visit Jesus—God's rescue plan for the world. When you think you're unimportant, remember: God thinks you're worth so much that he sent Jesus to rescue you.

Praise TV

O little town of Bethlehem (SOF: 420) or
From heaven you came, helpless babe (KS: 62)

Newshound

Newshound reminds the children that Mary and Joseph had no house to live in when Jesus was born. What other kind of people don't have anywhere to live? Refugees, the homeless and people who don't have a proper home may need our help this Christmas. Use material from Shelter (www.shelter.org.uk) or Crisis (www.crisis.org.uk) to illustrate.

Praise TV

See him lying on a bed of straw (KS: 291)

Runabout!

 As before, for each question, the announcer's assistants hold up cards, each showing one of two possible answers. The announcer asks a question and shouts 'Go!' The children run to the card showing what they think is the correct answer. They can then change their minds as the host shouts 'Runabout now!' Once they've made their final decision, reveal the answer. Children who get it wrong are out. At the end of

Dear Jesus, thank you that you were born to save us. Thank you that your death on the cross means we can all be rescued. Help us remember those who, just like you on that first Christmas, are without a proper home. Amen.

Praise TV

We three kings (from *Carols for Children*)

Launchpad song plays as the congregation leaves.

the quiz, the remaining children split into two teams. Each is given fragments of a different Bible verse. They race to rearrange the words, each helped by an assistant. Prizes are awarded, and the congregation learns both verses.

1. What sort of model did the contestants on *Make-it challenge* make?
   Correct: Nativity
   Wrong: Aeroplane

2. Who paid for the window that Bobby broke?
   Correct: Katie
   Wrong: Mickey

3. Who visited Jesus first?
   Correct: The shepherds
   Wrong: The wise men

4. Where did Mary and Joseph stay when Jesus was born?
   Correct: In a stable
   Wrong: In bed and breakfast

Key verses
He was wounded and crushed because of our sins; by taking our punishment, he made us completely well.
ISAIAH 53:5

God loved the world so much that he gave his only Son, so that everyone who believes in him may not die but have eternal life.
JOHN 3:16 (GNB)

Soap Street 3

 Cast
Bobby
Sheryl
Mickey
Jim
Katie

 Props
Two large plants and sign saying 'Soap Street Church' to indicate a church garden
Football

 Sound effects
Theme tune
Breaking glass

Play theme music. Enter Sheryl and Bobby.

BOBBY:	That was cool, Mum.
SHERYL:	It was, Bobby. I'm glad we met your friend Katie and her dad. I've enjoyed coming to church these past few weeks.

Enter Mickey with football.

MICKEY:	All right, mate. All right, Mrs W.
SHERYL:	*(Pointedly)* Good morning, Mickey.
MICKEY:	What you doing?
BOBBY:	Nothing.
SHERYL:	We've just been to church, Mickey. You should come with us.
MICKEY:	No way. My dad says it's a load of rubbish.
SHERYL:	Your dad should try it himself.
MICKEY:	He watches the footie on cable on Sundays. Do you want to play football, Bobby?
BOBBY:	Can I, Mum?
SHERYL:	I suppose so, Bobby, but don't mess up those clothes. Go and play in the park, though, not here. And make sure you're back in time for lunch.
BOBBY:	OK, Mum. See you later. *(Sheryl exits)* Come on, Mickey, let's go.
MICKEY:	Can't we just play here?
BOBBY:	Mum said we had to go to the park.
MICKEY:	It'll be OK.
BOBBY:	I don't know.

Mickey drops ball and dribbles it around Bobby. After a moment, Bobby joins in, chasing Mickey to get ball. Bobby tackles him and gets the ball. He approaches Mickey as if bearing down on goal.

Reproduced with permission from *Launchpad* published by BRF 2004 (1 84101 326 9)

BOBBY:	Here comes Bobby Watson. He's running rings round these defenders! He's unstoppable! But will he take on the big United keeper?

He stops abruptly in front of Mickey.

MICKEY:	Go on, then, have a shot!

Bobby steps back as far as he can go, perhaps back into congregation, then does long run-up before kicking the ball offstage. Both boys follow the path of the ball with their eyes, then flinch at sound of breaking glass.

MICKEY:	Blimey, Bobby, you've broken that window!
JIM:	*(From offstage)* Oi! What's going on?
MICKEY:	Right, I'm off! See you later, Bobby!

Mickey runs off.

BOBBY:	*(Shouts after him)* Mickey, where are you going?

Enter Jim and Katie.

JIM:	What's going on, Bobby?
BOBBY:	Er… well, you see… *(Speaks quickly and guiltily)* I was playing with Mickey, and I wanted to be the striker, and I had a shot, and Mickey was the goalie and and, I'm really sorry… *(Hangs his head)*
JIM:	You've broken a window! *(Bobby nods)* You'll have to clear up the mess and pay for the damage.
KATIE:	How much will that cost, Dad?
JIM:	At least a hundred quid.
BOBBY:	*(Looks up)* A hundred!
JIM:	Can you afford that, Bobby?
BOBBY:	I'll pay it out of my pocket money.
JIM:	How much do you get?
BOBBY:	Two quid a week.
JIM:	So it will take you twelve months to pay off.
BOBBY:	Twelve months? That's for ever! I'll never finish paying it back.
KATIE:	I've got enough in my bank account. I could pay it for you, Bobby.
BOBBY:	Would you really do that for me?
KATIE:	Course I would. I'm your friend.

Theme music to end.

Reproduced with permission from *Launchpad* published by BRF 2004 (1 84101 326 9)

He was wounded and
crushed because of our sins;
by taking our punishment,
he made us completely well.

ISAIAH 53:5

God loved the world so
much that he gave his only
Son, so that everyone who
believes in him may not die
but have eternal life.

JOHN 3:16 (GNB)

Launchpad theme song

CHORUS:

We're gonna take off, fly high in the sky.
Hey! Hey! We're on the Launchpad!
We're gonna find out what it's all about.
Hey! Hey! We're on the Launchpad!

VERSE 1:

Look in the Bible and what do you see?
God's love appearing throughout history.
There's goodies and baddies, there's happy and sad,
But stories of God's love will make you feel glad.

Chorus…

VERSE 2:

People messed up but our God had a plan,
He came to earth and he lived as a man,
Two thousand long years have since come and gone,
But Jesus' love for us keeps going strong.

Chorus…

VERSE 3:

God's love is for you and it is for me,
But many people aren't able to see
The wonderful things that our God has done
So let's go and share the good news of his Son.

FINAL CHORUS:

We're gonna take off, fly high in the sky.
Hey! Hey! We're on the Launchpad!
We're gonna find out what it's all about.
Hey! Hey! We're on the Launchpad!
Hey! Hey! We're on the Launchpad!
Hey! Hey! We're on the LAUNCHPAD!

Launchpad theme song

Words: Mark Rodel
Music: Kevin Golledge

I will search for my lost sheep

VERSE 1:

When David was a shepherd boy,
He cared for his father's flock,
When danger came, he protected them,
With staff, and sling and rock.
Both night and day he stayed with them,
His voice was always kind.
If they strayed away, he searched for them,
Leaving the rest behind:

CHORUS:

I will search for my lost sheep,
I will take good care of them,
I will save them from all the places
Where they were scattered on that dark day.
I will bandage the wounded ones,
And bring back those that have strayed away.

VERSE 2:

When all of us had turned away
From the laws that he had given,
God gave his prophets the words to say
About how we were living:
'You are my sheep, the flock I feed,
Won't you return to me?
To keep my laws you need my love,
Oh, will you ever see?'

Chorus…

VERSE 3:

Then Jesus came to find the lost,
To share the Father's love.
Now we know just what love cost
Our Lord from high above.
He felt our pain, he knew our fear,
Our lonely tears he cried,
To find the lost, he came so near,
To save us all, he died:

Chorus…

VERSE 4:

Now Jesus is the good shepherd,
He cares for his father's flock,
When danger comes, we're always safe,
He is a solid rock.
Both night and day he stays with us,
His spirit's always near.
If you stray away, just call on him,
You know he'll always hear:

Chorus…

I will search for my lost sheep

Words: Mark Rodel
Music: Kevin Golledge

search for my lost sheep, I will take good care of them, I will save them from all the pla-ces,_____ Where they were scat-tered on__ that dark day. I will ban-dage the woun-ded ones, And bring back those that have strayed a - way.

Look into my heart, Lord

Chester sings as Samuel. The service leader sings as God.
The two chorus parts are sung simultaneously.

INTRODUCTION:

(Samuel)
I have come to offer a sacrifice,
Purify yourselves and come with me.
For Saul has had to pay the price,
Of his pride and his stupidity.
Now God will choose his people a new king,
And one of Jesse's sons will be the man.
Now they're before me, standing,
God will show us all what is his plan.

VERSE 1:

(Samuel)
Here is Eliab, Jesse's eldest son,
This is just the one that I would choose.
He's so strong and tall and handsome,
He must be the one to fill Saul's shoes.

CHORUS:

(Samuel)
Surely this is the man,
See how tall and handsome he is.
Surely this is the man,
See how tall and handsome he is.

(God)
You look at the outside, but I look within.
You see what you want to see, but I see the sin.
You look at the outside, but I look within.
You see what you want to see, but I see the sin.

VERSE 2:

(Samuel)
Abinadab, Shammah, it is none of them,
They would be the ones that I would choose.
They were strong and tall and handsome,
One of them must surely fill Saul's shoes.

CHORUS:

(Samuel)
Surely this is the man,
See how tall and handsome he is.
Surely this is the man,
See how tall and handsome he is.

(God)
You look at the outside, but I look within.
You see what you want to see, but I see the sin.
You look at the outside, but I look within.
You see what you want to see, but I see the sin.

VERSE 3:

(Samuel)
All of Jesse's sons but one I now have seen,
And the one that's left is just a boy.
Here he comes from the fields where he has been,
Could he be the one, your people's joy?

CHORUS:

(God)
Surely this is the man,
See how full of grace he is.
Surely this is the man,
See how full of grace he is.

(Samuel)
I looked at the outside, but you look within.
Now I see what you see, that your Spirit's with him.
I looked at the outside, but you look within.
Now I see what you see, that your Spirit's with him.

VERSE 4:

(Samuel)

So God chose for his people a new king,
And Jesse's youngest son, he is the man.
Now David is before me, standing,
God has shown us all what is his plan.

CHORUS:

(God)
Surely this is the man,
See how full of grace he is.
Surely this is the man,
See how full of grace he is.

(Samuel)
Look into my heart, Lord, what do you see?
Search in ev'ry part, Lord, purify me.
Look into my heart, Lord, what do you see?
Search in ev'ry part, Lord, purify me.

Reproduced with permission from *Launchpad* published by BRF 2004 (1 84101 326 9)

Look into my heart, Lord

Words: Mark Rodel
Music: Kevin Golledge

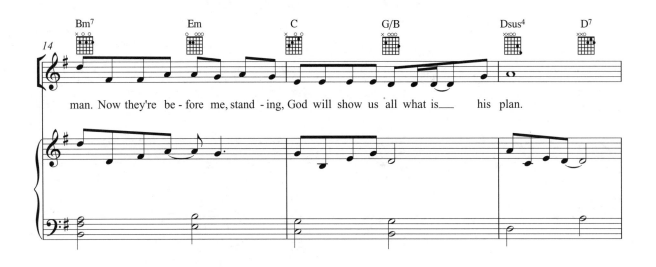

man. Now they're be - fore me, stand - ing, God will show us all what is__ his plan.

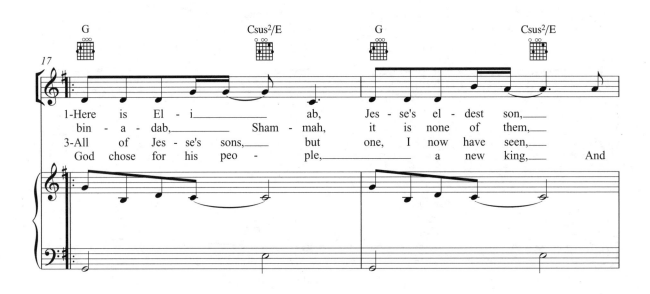

1-Here is El - i_____ ab, Jes - se's el - dest son,__
bin - a - dab,_____ Sham - mah, it is none of them,__
3-All of Jes - se's sons,__ but one, I now have seen,__
God chose for his peo - ple,_____ a new king,__ And

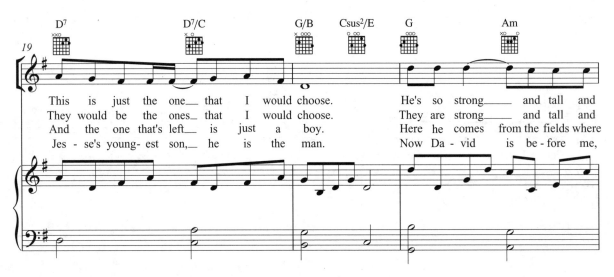

This is just the one__ that I would choose. He's so strong__ and tall and
They would be the ones_ that I would choose. They are strong__ and tall and
And the one that's left__ is just a boy. Here he comes from the fields where
Jes - se's young - est son, he is the man. Now Da - vid is be - fore me,

One giant leap

In the verses, Chester sings the bold parts, the service leader those in normal print.
Both should sing the chorus with the congregation.

VERSE 1:
The heathens on one hill: the Jews on another,
Shoulder to shoulder: each man with his brother
The Philistine champion: strides into sight,
Jews look to each other: and cry out with fright:
'This man is a giant: he knows no fear.
Just look at his armour: the size of his spear.
It's as thick as the bar: on a weaver's loom.
Surely Goliath: will bring us our doom.'

CHORUS:
And it's one giant leap
From shepherd to king,
With God on your side,
And a stone in your sling.
He'll give you the victory,
Just trust in the Lord.
His Spirit is sharper
Than the giant's sword.

VERSE 2:
Ev'ry morning Goliath: showed off his great might,
He challenged God's people: to give him a fight.
But they were too scared: though his threats made them mad
'Til out of the camp: came a young shepherd lad.
'I'll fight the giant': said David to Saul,
'This heathen is cursing: the God of us all.
And just as I killed both: the lion and bear
God will help me defeat him: he'd better beware.'

Chorus…

Reproduced with permission from *Launchpad* published by BRF 2004 (1 84101 326 9)

VERSE 3:

Then David ran forward: from out of the crowd.
Goliath just laughed: and he shouted out loud:
'Do you think I'm a dog: that you come with a stick?
You lot and your god: you make me feel sick.'
David kept coming: 'I'm ready to fight thee,
I come in the name of: the Lord God Almighty.
I will defeat you: now you mark my words:
You and your men: I will feed to the birds.'

Chorus…

VERSE 4:

David reached in his bag: and he pulled out a rock.
Goliath was in for: a mighty big shock.
The sling swung around: and then David let fly.
The stone hit the giant: he let out a cry.
David's first shot hit him: hard in the head.
He fell to the ground: he was stone-cold dead.
When the Philistines saw it: they all ran away,
And God gave his people: the vict'ry that day.

Chorus… (twice)

One giant leap

Words: Mark Rodel
Music: Kevin Golledge

(Voice 1 : Voice 2)

Reproduced with permission from *Launchpad* published by BRF 2004 (1 84101 326 9)

Saul has killed his thousands

VERSE 1:
'King Saul has killed his thousands,
David his tens of thousands,'
Full of joy, the people sang.
'For David: tens of thousands,
For me, it's only thousands,'
Through the palace, Saul's shouts rang.
The king was in a jealous rage,
'This boy has stolen centre stage.'
In David came, his harp to play.
'I'll throw my spear at him,' thought Saul,
'I will pin him to the wall.'
But David escaped and ran away.

CHORUS:
Jonathan, the king's own son,
Was full of love for David.
He could see he was the one
God had chosen to be king.

VERSE 2:
Saul of David was afraid,
So a wicked plan he made,
He would get the young man killed.
'I'll let you wed my daughter
If you will go and slaughter
A hundred heathens, I'd be thrilled!'
David and his men returned.
Two hundred heathens, Saul then learned,
Had met their end at David's hand.
'How can I protect my throne?
I'll go and kill him at his home!
There's only one king of this land!'

Chorus…

VERSE 3:
David's wife helped him to flee.
Saul would show him no mercy.
He ran till he was out of breath.
'What have I done wrong,' he said,
'That the king should want me dead?
I'm just a step away from death.'
David's friend came down his way,
Said that he should run away.
To part like this was such a shame.
They wept and kissed and said 'goodbye',
Swore their love would never die.
Their lives would never be the same.

Chorus… (twice)

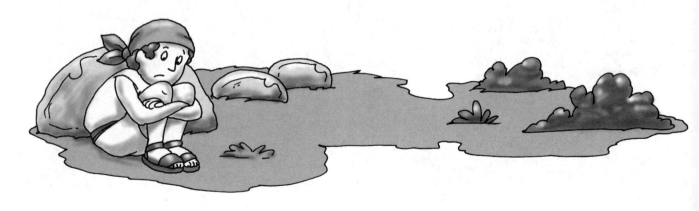

Saul has killed his thousands

Words: Mark Rodel
Music: Kevin Golledge

David's lament

Based on 2 Samuel 1:19–27.

VERSE 1:

On the hills of Israel, our leaders are slain,
The bravest of our soldiers battled in vain.
Don't let the Philistines hear of this news,
In the battle they've killed the king of the Jews.

CHORUS:

May no rain fall, no dew distil
On the fields atop Gilboa's hill.
For there the shields of the brave do lie,
Oh why should the Lord's anointed king die?
The shield of Saul: no more polished with oil.
His son's deadly bow: useless now on the soil.
And how I grieve for thee,
Jonathan, my friend, my brother.
The love you had for me
Was better than any other.
Oh, the love you had for me:
How wonderful, how wonderful,
My friend and my brother.

VERSE 2:

King Saul and his son, so wonderful and dear.
Together in life, in their death they were near.
Swifter than the eagles, like lions they were strong.
The heathens must pay for this terrible wrong.

Chorus…

VERSE 3:

Oh women of Israel, mourn for your king.
Weep now for Saul, this lament you should sing.
He clothed you in scarlet, adorned you with gold.
May the story of Saul for ever be told.

Chorus…

Reproduced with permission from *Launchpad* published by BRF 2004 (1 84101 326 9)

David's lament

Words: Mark Rodel
Music: Kevin Golledge

Chester's medley

CHORUS:
And it's one giant leap
From shepherd to king,
With God on your side,
And a stone in your sling.
He'll give you the victory,
Just trust in the Lord.
His Spirit is sharper
Than the giant's sword.

VERSES:
When David was a shepherd boy,
He cared for his father's flock,
When danger came, he protected them
With staff and sling and rock.
Both night and day he stayed with them,
His voice was always kind.
If they strayed away, he searched for them,
Leaving the rest behind:

I will search for my lost sheep,
I will take good care of them.
I will save them from all the places
Where they were scattered on that dark day.
I will bandage the wounded ones,
And bring back those who have strayed away.

Chorus (And it's one giant leap…)

Reproduced with permission from *Launchpad* published by BRF 2004 (1 84101 326 9)

VERSES:

So God chose for his people a new king,
And Jesse's youngest son, he is the man.
Now David is before me, standing;
God has shown us all what is his plan.

(Samuel)

Surely this is the man,
See how full of grace he is.
Surely this is the man,
See how full of grace he is.

(God)

I looked at the outside, but you looked within.
Now I see what you see,
That your Spirit's with him.
I looked at the outside, but you look within.
Now I see what you see,
That your Spirit's with him.

(Rap this verse)

David reached in his bag and he pulled out a rock.
Goliath was in for a mighty big shock.
The sling swung around and then David let fly.
The stone hit the giant, he let out a cry.
David's first shot hit him hard in the head.
He fell to the ground, he was stone-cold dead.
When the Philistines saw it, they all ran away,
And God gave his people the vict'ry that day.

(Sing)

The king was in a jealous rage,
'This boy has stolen centre stage.'
In David came, his harp to play.
'I'll throw my spear at him,' thought Saul,
'I will pin him to the wall.'
But David escaped and ran away.

Reproduced with permission from *Launchpad* published by BRF 2004 (1 84101 326 9)

Jonathan, the king's own son,
Was full of love for David.
He could see he was the one
God had chosen to be king.

Chorus (And it's one giant leap…)

VERSE:
May no rain fall, no dew distil
On the fields atop Gilboa's hill.
For there the shields of the brave do lie,
Oh why should the Lord's anointed king die?
The shield of Saul: no more polished with oil.
His son's deadly bow: useless now on the soil.

Chorus (And it's one giant leap…) (twice)

Chester's medley

Words: Mark Rodel
Music: Kevin Golledge

God gave his peo - ple: the vic - t'ry that day.

The king was in__ a jea - lous rage, 'This boy has sto__ - len cen - tre stage.' In

Da - vid came,__ his harp to play.__ 'I'll throw my spear__ at him,' thought Saul,

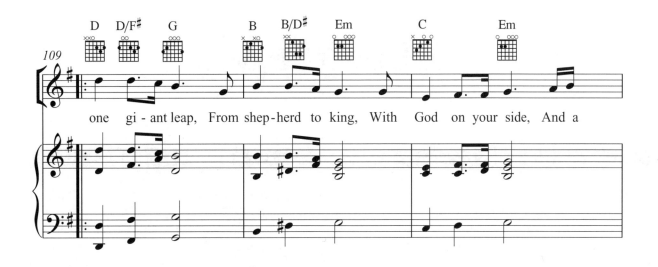

one gi-ant leap, From shep-herd to king, With God on your side, And a

stone in your sling. He'll give you the vic-tor-y, Just trust in the Lord. His

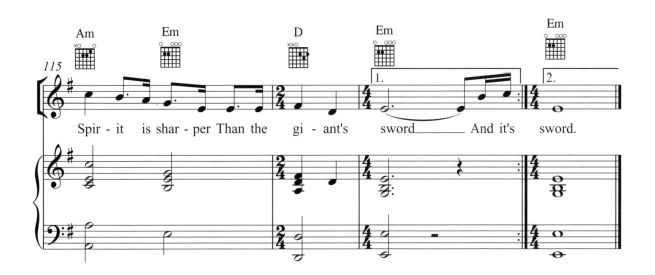

Spir-it is shar-per Than the gi-ant's sword____ And it's sword.

Bibliography

SONGS

Carols for Children (Macmillan, 1998)
Kidsource (Kevin Mayhew, 1999)
Kidsource 2 (Kevin Mayhew, 2002)
Songs of Fellowship (Kingsway, 1991)
Songs of Fellowship 2 (Kingsway, 1991)
Songs of Fellowship for Kids (Kingsway, 1998)
The Big Book of Spring Harvest Kids' Praise (ICC/Spring Harvest, 2000)

DRAMA AND ACTIVITIES

Bailey, John, *Worship!* (National Society/Church House Publishing, 1999)

Burbridge, Paul, and Watts, Murray, *Time to Act* (Hodder and Stoughton, 1979)

Burbridge, Paul, and Watts, Murray, *Lightning Sketches* (Hodder and Stoughton, 1981)

Burbridge, Paul, and Watts, Murray, *Red Letter Days* (Hodder and Stoughton, 1986)

Butterworth, Nick, and Inkpen, Mick, *Animal Tales* (Marshall Pickering, 1999)

Gardner, Jacqui, and Leonard, Chris, *The Road to Easter* (BRF, 2000)

Hopwood, Dave, and Hopwood, Lynn, *Telling Tales* (CPAS, 1997)

Hopwood, Dave, and Hopwood, Lynn, *Telling Even More Tales* (CPAS, 2000)

Leach, Chris, *100 Worship Activities for Children* (Kingsway, 2000)

Merrell, Judith, *101 Ideas for Creative Prayer* (Scripture Union)

Murrie, Diana, and Bruce, Hamish, *Worship through the Christian Year: All-Age Resources for the Three Year Lectionary: Year A* (National Society/Church House Publishing, 1998)

Murrie, Diana, and Bruce, Hamish, *Worship through the Christian Year: All-Age Resources for the Three Year Lectionary: Year B* (National Society/Church House Publishing, 1999)

Neilands, Lynda, *50 Stories for Special Occasions* (Kingsway, 1998)

★ ★ ★ ★ ★ ★ ★

Other resources from Barnabas

REF 1 84101 250 5, £11.99

This innovative drama and activities resource is ideal for use in school assemblies, the classroom or small group, holiday clubs and church services. Aimed primarily at 7-11s, the drama presents the message of Luke's Gospel in ten episodes, with an allegorical futuristic sci-fi theme. Each unit includes full script with photocopy permission, shortened version of the full script suitable for children to perform, talk outlines (some suitable for assemblies, some for small groups), quick questions to recap the drama, Bible passages written out in full, Bible story suggestion, activities, crafts, games, suggested songs and prayers.